GARY MITCHELL

Gary Mitchell was born and still lives in Rathcoole, North Belfast. He began his writing career in 1991 with *The World, the Flesh and the Devil*, which won the BBC Radio Drama Young Playwrights Festival, and since 1993 has been commissioned by BBC Radio 4 and Radio 3 to write a further eleven plays, including a three-part series about the RUC called *Dividing Force*. Single plays include *A Tearful of Dreams*, *Poison Hearts*, *Stranded*, *Drumcree* and *Independent Voice* – the first play by a writer from Northern Ireland to win the Stewart Parker Award, in 1994. He also co-wrote *Mandarin Lime* with Jimmy Murphy. His first stage play was *Independent Voice*, produced in 1993 by Tinderbox Theatre Company. Since then he has worked with Point Fields Theatre Company on *Alternative Future* and with Replay Theatre Company on *That Driving Ambition* and *Sinking*. *In a Little World of Our Own* was performed at the Peacock Theatre, Dublin, before embarking on one of the most successful tours of Ireland's theatre in recent times, going on to receive awards for Best New Play of 1997, Best Director (Conal Morrison) and Best Supporting Actor (Lalor Roddy) at the first Irish Theatre Awards. In 1998 *Tearing the Loom* was playing at the Lyric Theatre, Belfast, as *In a Little World of Our Own* opened in London at the Donmar Warehouse. Work in progress includes the provisional titles *As the Beast Sleeps* for the Peacock, *Energy* for the Playhouse, Londonderry, and, for the Royal National Theatre, London, a new play, *Trust*, following his appointment as Resident Playwright. His documentaries and screenplays for television include *Made in Heaven* in 1997 and *Red, White and Blue* in January 1998, both for the BBC, with *Enlightenment* for RTE scheduled for later in 1998.

Other Titles in this Series

GARY MITCHELL

Tearing the Loom
and
In a Little World of
Our Own

NICK HERN BOOKS

LONDON

A Nick Hern Book

Tearing the Loom and *In A Little World of Our Own*
first published in Great Britain in 1998
as an original paperback by Nick Hern Books Limited,
14 Larden Road, London W3 7ST

Tearing the Loom and *In A Little World of Our Own*
copyright ©1998 by Gary Mitchell

Gary Mitchell has asserted his moral rights as author
of this work

Cover image reproduced by kind permission of the
Lyric Theatre, Belfast. Copyright © Nineteen Twenty

Typeset by Country Setting, Woodchurch, Kent TN26 3TB

Printed in England by Athenaeum Press Ltd.,
Gateshead, Tyne and Wear

ISBN 1 85459 403 6

A CIP catalogue record for this book is available from
the British Library

IN A LITTLE WORLD OF OUR OWN

Thanks to Sandra and Chuck Mitchell
– my Mum, Dad and family –
Stuart Graham, Christopher Fitzsimon
Judy Friel, Conal Morrison
and Patrick Mason.

And special thanks to Carol.

In a Little World of Our Own was first performed in the Peacock auditorium at the Abbey Theatre, Dublin. First preview was on 6 February 1997; opening night was 12 February. The cast, in order of appearance, was as follows:

WALTER	Lalor Roddy
RAY	Stuart Graham
RICHARD	Marc O'Shea
GORDON	Sean Kearns
DEBORAH	Andrea Irvine

Director   Connall Morrison
Designer   Kathy Strachan
Lighting   Tony Wakefield
Stage Director   Colette Morris
Assistant Stage Director   Catriona Behan
Sound   Dave Nolan

The play returned to the Peacock on 13 August 1997 and went on tour North and South of the border with Stephen Kennedy playing RAY, Dan Gordon as GORDON and Eileen McCloskey as DEBORAH. Other cast remained the same.

The London premiere by The Foundry Theatre Company was at the Donmar Warehouse as part of the 1998 Four Corners Season. It played from 3 to 7 March. The cast was as follows:

WALTER	Lorcan Cranich
RAY	Stuart Graham
RICHARD	Colin Farrell
GORDON	Paul Hickey
DEBORAH	Helen McCory

Director   Robert Delamere

ACT ONE

Living room, early evening.

WALTER *is wearing plain black trousers, a shirt and tie, complete with UDA tie-pin, a cardigan and plain black shoes and socks.* RAY *is wearing jeans, t-shirt and DM's.* WALTER *gives* RAY *an envelope, which he tears open and takes money from, placing the money in his pocket and the envelope in the bin.*

RAY. Whose is the Chocolates?

WALTER. They're yours.

RAY. How's that?

WALTER. Mrs. Wilson gave me them, you know, a job well done and all that.

RAY. I suppose you've ate all the purple ones?

WALTER. I haven't touched them, actually.

RAY (*he takes the box and after opening it searches out a sweet with purple wrapper*). Did you explain to her about why we couldn't get all her stuff back?

WALTER. She understands. She's just so grateful that you were able to get what you got.

RAY. Did you tell her about Monroe?

WALTER. What about him?

RAY. I want people to know, Walter. That every time I try to get something done, I have this guy Monroe holding me back. Him and his non-violent crowd were all over me again this time. And I'm telling you, I'm not fucking happy about it. I want him off my back for good, Walter. For ever.

WALTER. No-one can deliver that, Ray. He's a powerful man.

RAY. I never thought I'd see the day when men like Monroe would be considered powerful. The world's gone fucking mad. Pricks like Monroe are just shit. What people don't understand is this. The world is a violent place. We know that better than anybody. Whether it's dealing with the IRA or dealing with petty theft or glue sniffing. Whatever. Namby-pamby ways don't get results.

WALTER. Everybody has their own way of doing things, Ray.

RAY. I've got a box of Roses from an old woman whose house has been burgled three times by the same boys. Now, Monroe and his people, they had first go. And when Monroe's talking and philosophying didn't work they called for us, Walter. Now, be fair, I always let you give them their last chance, but at the end of the day, what have we learnt? This box of Roses says my way works. See, I'm not just talking about beating people up. Doing people over. I'm talking about common sense. We haven't just helped Mrs. Wilson. We've helped everybody. Even those young fellas.

WALTER. I don't think they would see it that way. Especially when you were beating them with a hammer.

RAY. Time tells its own story. Years from now, when those young fellas have grown, they'll look back and realise that they could have been going to prison for years. They could've learnt things in prison, worse things. And they could've returned to the streets worse and tried to do bigger jobs, got caught again and ended up spending most of their time in and out of prison. I saved them from that. A few broken bones and bruising will be forgotten about in a couple of months. And they won't do it again. And who knows maybe they'll see things different, maybe they'll meet a girl, fall in love, settle down. Live lives.

WALTER. I doubt it.

RAY. But you don't know, Walter. Think about Curly Williams, think about Bap Higgins. They were bad boys.

WALTER. But Ray the main thing is, Monroe isn't going to go away. No matter what you say about your ways and his ways. People like him and people respect him. Not just ordinary people, money people and we need all the money we can get.

RAY. It's about the rights and wrongs of punishments, Walter. It's not about money.

WALTER. Everything's about money, Ray.

RAY. But it doesn't have to be. When this all started it wasn't about money. When you started and when I started we didn't start for money. We started and we're still here because we believe in what we're doing. Monroe doesn't bring the money into us. Monroe takes the money out and uses it to promote his own political agenda. But the UDA is not, and was never intended to be, a political party.

WALTER. That's right, Ray, but that's politics and if you ask me we're better off staying out of it.

RAY. All of us. Monroe not least of all.

WALTER. I'm not arguing with you. All I'm saying is, there's nothing we can do about it.

RAY. Maybe not. But that's not the whole problem, he's made it personal now, as well. With his attitude over our Richard and his daughter.

WALTER. She's supposed to be going with a taig now, you know.

RAY. Is that true? She is for definite, going with a taig.

WALTER. Who can tell? I didn't even know she was going with your kid brother.

RAY. She wasn't actually going with our Richard, they were mates. We used to call her his girlfriend and he liked it, but he won't like this. No-one likes to see a girl they fancy going out with a taig. (*Pause.*) See, this is exactly what I'm talking about, Walter. Used to be a time when taigs were shit scared of walking anywhere near Rathcoole. They just wouldn't do it. And now, they seem to be turning up all over the place. And it's because of people like Monroe.

WALTER. Well now his daughter's going with the taig surely that means there won't be anymore trouble between you and him over Richard.

RAY. Not really. You see, I know about his wee jokes. (WALTER *is concerned.*) That's right. I have ears everywhere, Walter. I know what he's been saying.

WALTER. Drink talks.

RAY. What was it he said? Were you ever going to tell me, like? I know you were there, I know you heard him – and to be honest I'm disappointed that you would let him away with it.

WALTER (*humbly*). I just didn't want to start any more bother.

RAY. Tell me what he said. I want to hear it from you.

WALTER *fumbles a cigarette from his pack of twenty and begins to search his own pockets for his lighter.*

WALTER. I honestly . . . can't remember.

RAY. Don't smoke in here. (WALTER *puts the cigarettes away*.)
Now! I'll start you off. He'd rather his daughter went with . . .
Give me the punch line. Give me the punch line, Walter.
(WALTER *tries to hide,* RAY *stands*.) Give me the fucking
punch line.

WALTER. Went with a retard than a taig.

RAY. Sorry? What did you say?

WALTER. *He* said. *He'd* rather his daughter went with a retard
than a taig.

RAY (*hurt*). I can't believe you said that, Walter. How long have
we been friends?

WALTER. I didn't say it.

RAY. How long have you been welcome in my Mother's house?

WALTER. I never said it, Ray?

RAY. I heard you saying it there now.

WALTER (*nervous*). You asked me to tell you what he said.

RAY. Who else was there?

WALTER (*shrugs*). Lots of people.

RAY. Was Mrs. Wilson there?

WALTER. Mrs. Wilson? She's an old woman for God's sake,
what would she be doing in a club?

RAY. An old woman who would have slapped his face for him if
she had have been there.

WALTER. What good what that do?

RAY. Who laughed?

WALTER. What?

RAY. It was a good joke, who laughed?

WALTER. Nobody. A couple of people.

RAY. Did you laugh?

WALTER. No. No fucking way, Ray. I swear to God. I didn't.

RAY. There wasn't many laughed in our house. When my
brother was a little kid, I cursed God. Not for what he did to
him, but for what he did to me. Then my Ma sat me down
once and said, Richard was given this gift from God, this gift
that makes him special, this gift that will protect him

wherever he goes. But that was the old days, the old ways and he would have been all right then. Wouldn't he?

WALTER. Yeah.

RAY. He's sensitive. He's full of love.

WALTER. I know he is.

RAY. I'm telling you *he's* the gift. He's the gift to us and we don't even realise it.

WALTER. OK, Ray, let's clear the air. First of all, I swear to God, I was going to say something, but I just . . . ah,.

RAY. You just what?

WALTER. I just . . . I don't know. (RAY *turns away.*) I wanted to slap him, but I was afraid, alright. He's got me by the balls, but I didn't laugh. No matter how much he squeezes I won't laugh. I swear to God. Come on, Ray, have you never been afraid.

RAY. Oh, I've been afraid alright. At school, these big lads taking the piss out of me the whole day long because my brother had to go to a special school. Joke after joke after joke and then I slapped one, he didn't laugh no more, and then I slapped another, and he stopped laughing too. And then it got easier and easier. You tell Monroe he's got a slapping coming.

WALTER. Ray.

RICHARD *is making his way from upstairs to the living room.*

RAY. No more talking about it, here he comes.

WALTER. Just hear me out!

RAY. What did I say?

Enter RICHARD, *dressed identically to* RAY.

RICHARD (*sets his and mum's dinner plates and cups etc., on the table*). Hiya, Wally.

WALTER. Son.

RAY. Who left all this, you or my Ma?

RICHARD. My Ma. She didn't want any more. She said it was stinking actually.

RAY. And you ate all yours?

RICHARD. Yes.

RAY. I'm going to ask her.

RICHARD. She's sleeping.

RAY. I'll ask her when she wakes up then.

WALTER. I'm going to shoot on, Ray, alright?

RAY. Where are you for now?

RICHARD. Where's the cards?

RAY. Never mind cards, take that tray into the kitchen. Give them a rinse and load them up in the dishwasher.

RICHARD. Fuck sake.

RAY. Move!

RICHARD. I'm going.

> RICHARD *takes* RAY*'s empty plate with the rest and goes to the kitchen.*

RAY. So are you going to the club or what?

WALTER. I dare say I will, aye. Are you coming down later on yourself?

RAY. I might.

WALTER. Well, if you do, I'll be there and sure I'll see you right for drink and that.

RAY. Fair enough.

WALTER. I'll not shout up to your Mum, if she's sleeping. Tell her I was asking about her but.

> RICHARD *returns, searches and finds cards.*

RAY. No problem, Walter. Take it easy.

WALTER. Will do. See you Richard.

> *Exit* WALTER.

RAY. What are you doing?

RICHARD. Playing cards. Do you want a game?

RAY. Only if you shuffle them properly.

RICHARD. Do you want a game or not?

RAY (*takes a seat at the table*). If you've done the dishes, I'm in.

RICHARD. What are we playing – Poker?

RAY. Don't ignore me.

RICHARD. Look! Dishwashers do dishes. Card Sharks, play cards. Now, I'll ask you again. Do you want a game of cards or not?

RAY. (RAY's *approval of his younger brother's cheekiness is reflected in his smile.*) Deal!

RICHARD. What do you want to play for – matches?

RAY. I'll sort them. You can have all these. (*Divides a box of matches by giving approximately two-thirds to* RICHARD *and keeping a third for himself.*) Now, before we get into this. Show me your poker face. (RICHARD *tuts.*) You think I'm being funny. The most important part of the game is facial expressions, Richard. Now, run me through them.

RICHARD. I've got all the faces. But here's a new one, that you won't even know. (*Makes a strange smiling face.*) What's that mean?

RAY. It means we shouldn't be playing cards because you're out of your fucking tree.

RICHARD. Or am I bluffing?

RAY (*laughs lightly; proud*). You're improving.

RICHARD. OK. It's your turn to show me something. The lifting trick.

RAY. I've showed you this before.

RICHARD. So, show me it again.

RAY. Right! When do you have complete control of the deck?

RICHARD. When it's your deal.

RAY. Correct! Now, how many people are playing in this game?

RICHARD. Four.

RAY *throws four hands of five cards, face up into the centre of the table; as though a game has just finished.*

RAY. The first thing you do, is look at all the cards, quickly. Speed is the key. Make up your mind instantly. (*We don't realise that as he speaks to* RICHARD *he is already studying the cards.*) Tell me about distraction.

RICHARD. Keep people talking. Makes them feel relaxed and upsets their plans. Yes?

RAY (*joking*). Did you used to play in Vegas? (RICHARD *smiles*.) What's your name again?

RICHARD (*proudly; gesturing with his fingers*). Rich Fingers.

RAY. And how do you stop yourself from losing your rich fingers?

RICHARD. Easy! Don't tear the arse out of it.

RAY. Exactly! But you do want to give yourself a good chance of winning, but remember, it's better to lose the odd time than to lose the odd limb. Now pick up a card that you want. Then, grab three close by all in one move. (*Does so.*) Then your next card, same thing again and again. Now the rest just goes to the bottom. And you know you've got a good hand. (*Deals.*) Maybe not the winner – this time. But most times.

RICHARD. I love it. Know what one I like? Ace to the bottom. I use that all the time.

RAY. Show me how you shuffle the cards without changing the ones at the top.

RICHARD. Watch and learn. (*Does so.*)

RAY. Are you sure you didn't play in Vegas?

RICHARD *laughs. As he deals,* GORDON *and* DEBORAH *enter the house.* DEBORAH *goes upstairs immediately,* GORDON *enters the living room.* GORDON *is wearing a suit and tie with good shoes.*

GORDON. It's only us.

RICHARD. Jesus Christ.

GORDON. No, only us, I said, Richard.

RAY. Where's Deborah gone?

GORDON. She's away up to see my Ma.

RAY. My Ma's sleeping.

GORDON. She won't wake her, don't worry. She's not stupid.

RICHARD. What's she going out with you for then?

GORDON. That's enough out of you.

RICHARD. Fine by me, we've a game on here.

GORDON. Well can you finish it before she comes down? We want to talk to you.

RAY. We've only just started.

RICHARD. But don't worry it won't be long 'til I skin the pants off Raymondo here.

GORDON. Come on, Ray. You know how she feels about card games.

RAY. Why don't you go to her house, Gordon? They're all God Squaders, aren't they?

GORDON. Deborah likes praying with my Ma. And my Ma likes her coming over to sit and talk with. It's good company for her. If it wasn't for Deborah she'd be lying in that room on her own every day until Kingdom come.

RAY (*looks at cards – to* RICHARD). Did you change my cards? (*He did.*)

RICHARD *shakes his head.*

GORDON. Ray, we have to talk.

RAY. Do we? (*To* RICHARD.) Give me three. (*Places three cards on the table.*)

GORDON. We need to get things sorted out.

RICHARD. You're supposed to ask for two.

RAY. How do you know?

RICHARD. You've got three Queens. You only need two cards.

RAY. But I want three.

RICHARD. You're just doing that.

GORDON. Richard, can you give me a wee second here?

RICHARD. Hold on. (RICHARD, *looks up at the sky and pretends to ask Jesus.*) No. (*Sniggers.*)

RAY. Cards.

RICHARD *gives* RAY *two cards.*

GORDON (*approaches the table*). I say you can.

RICHARD (*points to imaginary figure, hovering above the table*). Jesus said I can't.

RAY. Another card please.

RICHARD. You only need two.

RAY. No I don't. (RICHARD *tuts.*) Card.

GORDON. Listen to me. We've got some stuff we need to talk about.

RICHARD. I'm not stopping you. (*Places his hand out on the table.*) Three kings, I win.

RAY. You can't win, you haven't given me my other card yet.

RICHARD. But you're just doing that because you know.

RAY. Is that what you're going to do in a real game? Know what that'll get you?

RICHARD. But they wouldn't do that in a real game.

RAY. What would you do if someone did, Richard?

RICHARD. They wouldn't.

GORDON. Look, I'll get Deborah to come down now, before you start another game. Just so as you know what to expect. I might as well tell you now. We've seen a house.

Pause.

RAY. I'm very happy for you. My deal.

GORDON. Is that it? You don't think we need to talk about this.

RAY. Gordon, there's no two people in the world more happy than me and him. You're getting married, you've found a house. You won't be staying here, neither will she.

RICHARD *laughs.*

GORDON. But what about my Ma? What about Richard?

RAY. What about them?

GORDON. All I'm saying is when Deborah comes down she might start talking about things.

RICHARD. No change there.

GORDON. Just let her talk. We can talk about it better when she goes home.

RAY. What are you trying to say?

GORDON. Just don't fly off the handle.

RAY. I might have to go out, anyway.

GORDON. Just remember this. Nothing's been decided. Where have you to go?

RAY. I might go over and have a wee word with Monroe.

GORDON. You don't need to talk to him. It was sorted. He thought Susan was here last night, or with Richard somewhere, but when he seen Richard sitting here with us, that was him. Happy enough.

RAY. I have to see him about something else and I might go and meet Walter for a drink. Either way, I won't be here.

GORDON. Well, hang on, let me just go and get Deborah and we'll kick things off a bit.

Exit GORDON.

RICHARD. Are you forgetting about something?

RAY. Like what?

RICHARD. How are you going to go for a drink with Walter, when you're taking me to the party?

RAY. It's not tonight, is it?

RICHARD. It is tonight. I've told you.

RAY. Right, don't panic. Settle yourself.

RICHARD. What are we going to do?

RAY. Are you going to be seeing Susan before the party, at it or after it or what?

RICHARD. I'm meeting her about seven.

RAY. No, there is no abouts, Richard. I want exact times. When are you starting and when are you finishing?

RICHARD. Seven.

RAY. And?

RICHARD. See what happens.

RAY. No! We don't see what happens. Eleven. Gordon'll be coming home from Church, if we're fast, we'll be in before he knows anything about it, alright?

RICHARD. Right, but you have to remember to stay out of sight. I don't want anybody seeing you.

RAY. Hey! Give me some credit. I'll leave you at Doonbeg Drive, I'll watch you from there and same thing coming back, I'll be there from a quarter to eleven, you come out whenever, but not after eleven. Is it a deal?

RICHARD. Deal.

RAY. Do the lifting trick.

RICHARD. What if this fella's there again?

RAY. The Catholic guy?

RICHARD. Aye.

RAY. There's nothing I can do about that. It's not my party, Richard.

RICHARD. What if he starts mucking about with Susan again but?

RAY. You stay well away from them. If Susan doesn't object, then . . . then that's up to her. (*Pause.*) Look, you and Susan's good mates, right, so, you have to work that one out for yourself, but, if Susan does object, then that's a different matter.

RICHARD. What do I do then?

RAY. Well, who's going to be at this party? Joe? Rab?

RICHARD. I don't know. Me and Susan, that's all I know. And probably this fella like, he seems to be always turning up everywhere now.

RAY. Is Susan going with this guy or what?

RICHARD. No. She goes with me.

RAY. Well, OK, then. If something happens and Susan looks unhappy about it, try to suss it out, like, properly. Ask her straight out, no don't. I tell you what, do you want me to sort this guy out for you? Make him not come back no more.

RICHARD. I don't know.

RAY. Well, here's what to do. You go and have a good time, keep away from him, do you hear me?

RICHARD. Yes, I'm listening.

RAY. Any sign of trouble. Any problems at all. You get up and you come out, right? Right? You come straight round to here, tell me and I'll sort it, right? Tell me what you're going to do.

RICHARD. What if you're out drinking with Walter?

RAY. I'll see Walter, all you have to do is come round here straight away, I'll be here, alright?

RICHARD. Right.

Enter DEBORAH *and* GORDON. DEBORAH *is beautifully made up. She is wearing a very pretty flowery dress, white high heels, flesh coloured tights.*

DEBORAH. She was still awake, she asked me to pray with her. I think she was really glad I came up to see her.

GORDON. That's good.

DEBORAH (*to* RICHARD). How's Richard?

GORDON. Richard!

RICHARD. What?

GORDON. Deborah's speaking to you.

RICHARD *ignores them.*

RAY. You've got some news for all of us, Deborah? Gordon here seems to think we've a lot of stuff that needs to be sorted out.

GORDON (*to* DEBORAH). About Richard and my Ma and all.

DEBORAH. The only news I have Ray, is we've found a house.

GORDON. And I was just thinking maybe Richard would want to have a wee look at it.

RICHARD. What for?

GORDON. Just to see what you thought about it.

Silence.

DEBORAH. Richard, would you like to come and see the house or not?

RICHARD. No.

GORDON. You should come and see it, Richard. You'll really like it. It's much bigger than this. And your room could be magical.

RICHARD. What room's my room?

GORDON. We haven't sorted anything out yet, but I was thinking maybe if we got this house, maybe you could come and stay with us.

RAY. What are you trying to say, Gordon?

GORDON. I'm not trying to say anything. I'm asking Richard if he wants to come and see this house. Do you want to come with us tonight, Richard? Just to have a look at it.

RICHARD. No.

DEBORAH. There's no big rush, we're only saying, if you want to have a look, you can.

GORDON. Why not?

RICHARD. Because I've got things to do.

GORDON. No you haven't.

DEBORAH. Do you think he should see it, Ray?

RAY. If he wants to.

RICHARD. I'm going to a party tonight.

>   RAY *reacts to* RICHARD *giving up the secret.*

GORDON. No you're not.

RICHARD. I am.

RAY. He is. It's been arranged for ages. I said he could go.

GORDON. What kind of party?

DEBORAH. Leave it Gordon, he can go and see the house some other time.

GORDON. What kind of party?

RICHARD. A party, party.

RAY. Don't worry I'm leaving him over and picking him up afterwards.

GORDON. Where is it?

RICHARD. None of your business where it is.

GORDON. It is my business.

RICHARD. Well I'll tell you where it isn't. It's not in your house.

GORDON. What's that supposed to mean?

RICHARD. It means what it means.

GORDON. Try talking sense, Richard, will you?

RICHARD. I am talking sense.

RAY. Can we move this on, Gordon. He's busy tonight, if you want him to see this house of yours, it'll have to be some other time.

GORDON. Right, fair enough. If that's the way you want it.

RICHARD. I don't care I never see your house, Gordon.

GORDON. Listen, wee lad, you'll be seeing it tomorrow.

RICHARD. No, I won't.

DEBORAH. Gordon!

GORDON. Me and Deborah are going over tomorrow and you're going with us, alright?

RICHARD. I don't have to go with them, Ray. You said.

GORDON. Forget about what he said.

RAY. Gordon, settle yourself.

GORDON. Tell him, Ray.

RAY. Tell him what?

GORDON. Tell him he has to come with us.

RAY. But he doesn't.

GORDON. You're not thinking properly.

DEBORAH. Gordon, I think you're the one that isn't thinking properly.

GORDON. Things are happening, Ray. You're going to have enough on your plate just looking after my Ma. And what about when . . . something happens. Think about it.

RAY. I don't need to think about it, Gordon. I'm not the one who's leaving.

RICHARD. Neither am I.

DEBORAH. Can I just say something?

RAY. Go ahead.

GORDON. What is that – I'm not the one who's leaving – what is that?

DEBORAH. Gordon?

GORDON. Right.

DEBORAH. Are you listening, Richard?

RAY. Listen!

RICHARD. Go, hurry up.

DEBORAH. What Gordon's trying to say, Richard, is that we have found a house and we will be getting married and moving into it. The thing is, your brother loves you an awful lot. So much so, that he wants to get a house big enough so as you can come and live with us. Now, how permanent that is, is up to you. You can stay here whenever you want so long as you know you can also stay with us, again, whenever you want. Isn't that right, Gordon?

GORDON. No, that's not right.

DEBORAH. What's not right about it?

GORDON. He has to come and live with us. He can't stay here no more.

RAY. That's shite, Gordon.

RICHARD. That is shite. I'm staying here with Ray.

GORDON. Do you think so?

RICHARD. I fucking know so.

GORDON. Don't use that language in front of Deborah.

RICHARD. Fuck you.

> GORDON *is prevented from touching* RICHARD *by* RAY, *who simply stands in his way.*

RAY. Settle Gordon.

> GORDON *tries to get control of himself.*

RAY. He won't do it again and if he does I'll knock his cunt in.

DEBORAH. Gordon! You can't make him come with you.

GORDON. Can I not?

DEBORAH. No you can't.

RAY. This is where you have it all mixed up, Gordon, mate. You're just blowing it, here and now.

GORDON. Well, what do you suggest? Look at him. He's ungrateful. Have you any idea of the trouble I've gone to, just to give him this opportunity?

RAY. Settle yourself.

GORDON. You talk to him, Ray. He'll listen to you.

DEBORAH. It seems obvious to me, you're wasting your time, Gordon.

GORDON. Am I?

RICHARD. Yes you are. Me and Ray's staying together.

GORDON. But Ray can't look after you.

RICHARD. Ray?

RAY. What have I told you? It's up to you. He can't make you go and I can't make you stay.

RICHARD. Tell him that.

RAY. I don't need to tell him.

DEBORAH. Why don't you come over here, Richard and we'll have a wee talk?

RICHARD. No.

DEBORAH. Come on, Richard. We're only going to talk, now that Gordon's calmed down.

RICHARD (*throws his cards into the middle of the table and storms out*). No!

RAY. Hey!

GORDON. Will you go and get him, Ray?

DEBORAH. Will you talk to him?

RAY. I've said all I need to say.

GORDON. But it would be better if you talked to him about it. To let him know it's OK.

DEBORAH. Unless you think it's not OK. Do you Ray? I mean do you think you could cope yourself here, with your Mum and Richard?

RAY. I told you, I've said all I need to. (*Collects cards and tidies the playing area.*)

GORDON. He doesn't have to stay with us all the time.

RAY. He doesn't have to stay with you at all.

GORDON. What do you mean?

DEBORAH. Do you think he should stay here with you, Ray?

GORDON. Think about it Ray.

RAY. I'm going to go and make sure he's all right.

Exit RAY.

DEBORAH. Do you know what we should do?

GORDON. What?

DEBORAH. Pray. It's the only thing for it. If God wants Richard to stay with us, then it'll work out, but there's no point in us trying to make him do it, if it isn't God's will.

GORDON. What do you mean? Do you think maybe God wouldn't want him to stay with us?

DEBORAH. We have to pray about it.

GORDON. I don't know, Deborah.

DEBORAH. What?

GORDON. I'm not too good at praying. When I pray God doesn't speak to me or if he does, I don't know what he's saying. Everybody else seems to be able to understand him, but not me. I just talk and that's it.

DEBORAH. Do you want me to pray *for* you?

GORDON. What if God did answer me? What if he told me to do something that I didn't want to do, or I couldn't do, what then?

DEBORAH. Gordon. He wouldn't do that.

GORDON. What about Abraham?

DEBORAH. Exactly!

GORDON. See! That's what I mean. God asked him to kill his own son. Know what I mean? I would have just said no.

DEBORAH. Then God wouldn't ask you to do that. See? It's all to do with faith. You have to believe.

GORDON. But how do you believe?

DEBORAH. You pray and ask God to help you.

GORDON. Well, what if God asked me to leave our Richard here and told me that my Mum was going to die?

DEBORAH. I think we really need to pray, Gordon.

GORDON. I'm really sorry, Deborah, but not now. I really thought we could get this sorted out, if we could just get everybody to talk about it, properly. But we've no chance now. Not with this party.

DEBORAH. Well, when will it be over? – What kind of party does Richard go to?

GORDON. It's some wee girl's birthday or something. There's an empty house somewhere, somebody's parents are away and . . . It's not far from here. They think I don't know these things you see. They think I don't care.

DEBORAH. They know you care, Gordon. You're just not very good at showing it. It's the same as your problem with God and praying, you're not very good at explaining yourself.

GORDON. I know but Deborah it's like this. I'm the bad guy. You see I wouldn't have let him go to the party, you know. Our Ray but, he'll let him do anything. Know what I mean? But at the end of the day, where's Ray going to be when it really comes down? Like something goes wrong at this party, something happens and Richard gets hurt.

DEBORAH. But Richard's young, Gordon. He should be getting out more. A party or two could do him good. Instead of spending all his time sitting in here playing cards.

GORDON. No. He shouldn't. He should be here at night. Or when we get our place, he should be with us.

DEBORAH. Gordon!

GORDON. You don't understand, Deborah.

DEBORAH. I do understand.

GORDON. We're talking about a drinking party, full of wee lads and wee girls. I bet you that wee girl Monroe's going to be at it.

DEBORAH. What if she is? So what?

GORDON. Our Richard has serious problems with her. More with her Da, like.

DEBORAH. Richard fancies her. There's nothing wrong with that, Gordon. I'd be more worried if he didn't fancy anybody. Have you ever thought of that?

GORDON. She's not like anybody but, she's only fifteen for a start.

DEBORAH. I know her from the GB, Gordon. Everybody fancies her. Everybody. She was always being told to get her skirt fixed, she wore it so high. There was always a gathering of young fellas outside, just to get a look at her. And I'll tell you what, I don't ever remember hearing her telling them not to look. Know what I mean?

GORDON. I know exactly what you mean. I know exactly what kind of wee girl she is. That's why I'm worried.

DEBORAH. Don't be. What could possibly go wrong. You said it's not far from here. So everybody will know who Richard is. Everybody will know who Susan is. Everybody will know everybody and more than likely everybody will know your Ray. And that for me, would mean, we've got nothing to worry about. Where's your faith?

GORDON. Faith?

DEBORAH. Yes. Faith.

GORDON. I don't know.

DEBORAH. Well let's see if we can find it in church tonight. We can talk to Richard later on, when we come back.

GORDON. Are you going to come back here after church then?

DEBORAH. If you want me to, I will.

GORDON. Or do you think I should maybe try to talk to them myself or something?

DEBORAH. Maybe. You know. Maybe there's things they won't say in front of me.

GORDON. Like what?

DEBORAH. I'm just saying maybe.

GORDON. So, you don't want to come then?

DEBORAH. You're not listening, Gordon.

GORDON. Maybe we should just forget about it.

DEBORAH. What?

Silence.

Don't be getting comfortable. You can't make a statement like that and not explain it. Forget about what exactly?

GORDON. This house idea.

DEBORAH. Here we go again.

GORDON. I mean, what do we need a house for?

DEBORAH. Because we're getting married and we're going to need a place to live.

GORDON. We could live here.

DEBORAH. I don't think so.

GORDON. Think about it.

DEBORAH. I'd rather not. If you think for one minute that I'm going to get married and live here in this house with your Mum upstairs and your two brothers doing whatever it is they do, forget it. No chance. No way.

GORDON. But I can't just leave them. Not now, not like this.

DEBORAH. Why not? That's what people do. You're born into your family, you grow up, you get married and you leave home and start your own family. Isn't that what we decided?

GORDON. No. That's what you decided.

DEBORAH. Oh, so I'm the one who asked you to get married, am I?

GORDON. I didn't mean it like that.

DEBORAH. You better sort out what you do mean.

GORDON. Will you give me a break here?

DEBORAH. I'll give you a break. I'm going.

GORDON. Wait!

DEBORAH. I'll get my Da to drop me off at church. If you're there, I'll see you there and if not, well.

GORDON. Deborah, hold on. You know I can't leave until someone comes back.

DEBORAH. And where is everybody, Gordon? Where is everybody when you need them?

GORDON. Wait with me. We can go up and talk with my Ma.

DEBORAH. They're away, doing whatever they want. Why, Gordon? Because you're here, because you're the mug that's always going to be here.

GORDON. Well, it was kind of my own fault.

DEBORAH. It's your own fault because you won't stand up for yourself. What do you think they would do, if you weren't here? Do you think they'd go running off mad then?

GORDON. That's my problem, Deborah. I do.

DEBORAH. They wouldn't Gordon. They would be in here, doing what they have to do. They're doing this deliberately, Gordon. Can you not see that? You have to see it, Gordon. You have to leave here. Otherwise we've just wasted our time finding the house. Making all those plans, making all the arrangements. So you just let me know what you decide.

GORDON. Deborah?

Exit DEBORAH.

ACT TWO

Living room, late at night.

DEBORAH *is sitting at the table, it has been cleared.*
GORDON *brings* WALTER *into the living room, removing his old time peak cap and snorkel jacket.*

WALTER. That's a terrible night.

GORDON. But at least it's not raining. I always get soaked to death when it rains.

WALTER. Collecting like.

GORDON. What else?

DEBORAH. But at least it's an excuse for your *female* policy holders to offer you a cup of tea.

GORDON *smiles at* WALTER, *almost embarrassed.*

GORDON. The wee women on my book are dynamite. See if I didn't say no, I'd have tea coming out of my ears.

DEBORAH. Do you want a cup of tea, Walter?

GORDON *leaves with* WALTER'*s hat and coat.*

WALTER. I'm all right, I'm sorry to bother you at this time, actually. Only I seen the light on and thought Ray would have been sitting up. Are you off tomorrow? Today, even.

DEBORAH. No, I wish I was.

GORDON. You just caught us in time. I was just about to run Deborah home.

WALTER. I'm not interrupting anything, am I?

DEBORAH. No.

GORDON. So, what are you doing knocking people up at this time of the night, Walter?

WALTER. I was just saying I seen the light on.

GORDON. Ray's not in yet. Are you sure you don't want anything while you wait for him?

WALTER. No, I'm dead on. (*Pause.*) We've a bit of a problem.

GORDON. What kind of problem?

WALTER. Missing person.

DEBORAH. Who's missing?

WALTER. It's a young girl.

GORDON. What girl?

WALTER. Suzie Monroe.

DEBORAH. Her! Is she just missing or has she run away or something?

WALTER. Her Da doesn't think so and her Mum says she had no reason to run away.

GORDON. How long has she been missing?

WALTER. According to them, she went out with some friends and everything seemed fine. But she hasn't come home.

GORDON. Just tonight?

WALTER. She's only fifteen, Gordon.

DEBORAH. Have they spoke to her friends?

GORDON. I bet you she's staying with one of her friends. That'll be it.

WALTER. We've checked them all.

GORDON. I take it you've been on to the Police.

WALTER. The Police are doing their usual, not very much. Like most people, they seem to think she's just staying with a friend.

GORDON. Maybe she's got a new boyfriend.

DEBORAH. Maybe something *has* happened to her.

GORDON. Maybe you should start checking some of these wee lad's houses.

WALTER. That's a possibility.

GORDON. Do you want us to go out and have a look somewhere?

WALTER. No.

DEBORAH. We couldn't wake people up at this time of the night.

GORDON (*to* WALTER). Why not?

WALTER. Where's Richard?

GORDON (*hesitates*). This is ridiculous. Are you here to check on us, Walter?

WALTER. No.

DEBORAH. Check on who?

GORDON. Let me tell you something, Walter, all the fellas around here have a thing for that wee girl. Are you going to check on all of them?

WALTER. Not all of them wanted to run away with her.

GORDON. That was ages ago.

WALTER. But Monroe didn't like your Richard being anywhere near her.

GORDON. We know. He's caused enough trouble over it.

WALTER. He's just acting like any father would act. (*Quickly.*) That's what he would say.

GORDON. And now he reckons they've run off together.

DEBORAH. Richard's harmless, and he always does what he's told.

WALTER. Where is he anyway?

GORDON. Bed!

DEBORAH (*almost in time with* GORDON). Out!

WALTER. Which one is it?

DEBORAH. Listen, I'm going to have to go home. I've to open the shop in the morning and if the new shoe racks aren't organised properly by 9 o'clock, Hilary'll do her nut.

GORDON. You better phone your Da, I can't leave the house until Ray comes back.

DEBORAH. Right.

We hear RAY *and* RICHARD *entering the house.* GORDON *looks at* WALTER *as* RAY *enters the room, slowly followed by* RICHARD.

RAY. You not away home yet?

GORDON. We were waiting on you?

WALTER. I was just on my way, myself.

RAY. What's up, Walter? (*Quickly to* RICHARD.) Richard! Bed!

WALTER. Where were you's?

RAY *studies* GORDON *before replying.*

RAY. Richard was at a party, it ran late. I went over to make sure
he got home all right.

DEBORAH. Was it good?

RAY (*before* RICHARD *can answer*). Bed!

GORDON. Is the party just over there now?

WALTER. Who all was at this party?

DEBORAH. Was Susan Monroe at it?

RAY. What is this, twenty questions? What's the matter?

RICHARD. Ray?

RAY. Where'd I tell you to go?

RICHARD *goes to bed after everyone says goodnight.*

GORDON. Monroe's daughter's gone missing again.

RAY. She's not missing, she's all right.

RICHARD (*calling from upstairs*). I don't want to be on my
own.

RAY. I'll be up in a minute.

WALTER. I take it that means she was at this party.

RAY. You take it right. That's why our Richard's upset a bit. Is
my Ma sleeping?

DEBORAH. She's been sleeping for a while. What happened at
the party?

RAY. She left early with a fella called Michael.

WALTER. Is he the Catholic fella?

RAY. I think so.

WALTER. She's for it now.

DEBORAH. What do you mean?

WALTER. The state her Da was in, when I left him. He was one
seriously angry man. When he finds this out, God help her.
There's no telling what he might do.

RAY. He's only himself to blame.

WALTER. How come?

RAY. Think about it, Walter. I've been warning everybody about this for years and nobody would listen. In fact, as you know, Walter, it's Monroe himself, who has stopped me from doing anything about it. So, we'll see where his non-violent attitude gets him now.

DEBORAH. At least everything turned out all right in the end, eh Walter?

WALTER. For us anyway.

RAY. So are you hitting the road, Walter? I don't want anybody wakening my Ma up, know what I mean?

WALTER. No problem.

RICHARD *enters*.

GORDON. What's the matter, Richard?

RICHARD. Ray?

RAY. Where did I tell you to go?

RICHARD. What's Walter doing here? Is he looking for Susan?

RAY. Never mind about Walter.

DEBORAH. He was here to see us about something.

RAY. And he's leaving now anyway. So get back to your bed.

RICHARD. But I don't want to be on my own.

RAY. I'm going to be up in two seconds.

WALTER. Are you all right, son?

RAY. Fuck up, Walter. You're leaving.

WALTER. I was only asking, mate.

RAY. Well, fucking don't, alright?

GORDON. Ray, the fella was only asking a question.

RAY. Gordon why don't you take Deborah home now, and you can drop Walter off on the way?

GORDON. Because we've got things to talk about, remember?

RAY. We've got nothing to talk about.

DEBORAH. Come on, Gordon. This is obviously not a good time to talk.

GORDON. I'm not going anywhere until I see Richard's all right.

RAY. Richard sit over there and keep your mouth shut.

GORDON. Ray, will you wise up.

RAY. Hey, my Ma's in bed sleeping and I'd like to keep it that way. And I want to get him to bed and I want to get myself to bed. Now get her and get him and get out.

DEBORAH. Let's go Gordon.

GORDON. Who do you think you're talking to here?

RAY. Who am I talking to? I'm beginning to wonder because I don't see anybody moving.

WALTER. I'm going to walk on home.

RAY. At last.

RICHARD. Ray?

RAY. I'll deal with you in a minute.

RICHARD. Ray, Walter's doing something.

WALTER. I'm not doing anything.

GORDON. What do you think he's doing?

RICHARD. He's trying to make me say something about what happened. That's why he's asking questions.

RAY. Fuck up, Richard, I mean it now.

RICHARD. It's him.

RAY. Thought you were leaving, Walter.

WALTER. I am. I was only asking him if he was all right.

RICHARD. He's trying to make me say something about Susan.

GORDON. What?

DEBORAH. What about Susan?

RAY. What did I tell you?

RICHARD. I can't remember.

RAY. I told you to keep your mouth shut.

RICHARD. But it's him, he's asking questions and I can't remember what you told me to say.

WALTER. I'm not asking anything.

RAY. He's not asking you anything, Richard.

WALTER. I'm just going home, alright?

GORDON. Why would he be asking you questions about Susan?

RICHARD. She just fell, tell them Ray. It was the taig's fault, not ours.

RAY. I don't fucking believe you.

DEBORAH. What are you talking about?

GORDON. What's going on, Ray?

RAY. Are you fucking happy now?

WALTER. Hey! I never heard a thing. As far as I'm concerned . . .

RAY. Just fucking sit down, Walter. 'Til we get this sorted out.

WALTER. Whatever you say. And I mean that.

GORDON. What are you talking about Susan for, Richard?

RAY. Because he's a fucking big mouth, that's why.

RICHARD. I'm only saying she fell. I never said nothing about you.

GORDON. Thought you said Susan was OK.

RAY. She was when she left the party.

DEBORAH. Did something happen after that?

RAY. Not that it's any of your business, but yes, something did happen.

GORDON. What happened?

RICHARD. The taig was doing things to her and then he saw me and he hit me and then Ray came along and she fell.

WALTER. I don't really want to hear this, Ray. Would it not be better if I just went on my way? I'm not going to say nothing to anybody. You know, I'm all right like.

RAY. Just fuck up, Walter. Here's the score. Gordon, take Richard upstairs and make sure he's all right.

RICHARD. No, I want to stay with you, Ray.

RAY. I'll be up in a minute, I just want to sort things out first. Gordon, come on.

GORDON. No, I want to know what's happened here.

RAY. I'll tell you later, but I need to talk to Walter first.

DEBORAH. Go on, Gordon. Do what he says.

RICHARD. I'm staying with Ray.

RAY. Richard! If you don't start doing what you're told I'm not going to be able to protect you. Do you understand? You're going to be on your own when the bad men come.

GORDON. Don't be saying things like that.

RAY. It's true. Now, either you go with Gordon or I'm out of here and you can look after yourself.

RICHARD. I'm going, I'm going.

DEBORAH. Go Gordon.

Exit GORDON *and* RICHARD.

RAY. Right, listen to this, both of you. And listen carefully.

WALTER. Whatever you say.

DEBORAH. Has something happened to the wee girl, Ray?

RAY. Just listen to me Deborah. OK?

DEBORAH. OK.

RAY. This, wee girl, has been torturing our Richard for years. One minute she's his best friend and the next minute, she's not. Anyway, tonight she decided she's not. And she left the party with this taig fella, alright?

DEBORAH. What happened?

RAY. Well, I was supposed to meet Richard at eleven, but he didn't turn up. And nobody knew where he was or where he had gone. But everybody knew where Susan and the scumbag had gone. Up the Cave Hill. So I put two and two together and headed off after them and sure enough our Richard had followed them.

WALTER. Her Da will go mad when he finds this out.

RAY. I don't think so.

DEBORAH. Why?

RAY. Well, when I got there, this guy was acting the hard man with our Richard. So I lost my temper a bit and slapped him a few times and your woman she got all funny about talking shit and trying to get me to leave him alone and all. So, I stopped hitting him to take our Richard home, but Richard wanted to make sure she was all right, so he made me go back for her. And that was when I found her.

WALTER. What do you mean found her?

RAY. Well, I must have pissed this guy off big time and unfortunately being a yellow bastard he couldn't fight me so he took all his anger out on Susan.

WALTER. Did he rape her?

RAY. He might have, but that'll hardly matter.

DEBORAH. Why not?

RAY. Because I think he might have beaten her to death.

WALTER. You think.

RAY. Our Richard came on the scene. So, I had to get him out of there.

DEBORAH. And what did you do about her?

RAY. There was nothing I could do.

DEBORAH. What?

WALTER. Did you phone an ambulance?

DEBORAH. Did you phone the Police?

RAY. I can't.

WALTER. Ah, Ray.

DEBORAH. Is she still up there?

RAY. We have to let this thing take its course.

WALTER. What are you talking about?

RAY. Think about it.

DEBORAH. We have to phone somebody now.

RAY. No we don't.

WALTER. We probably really should, Ray.

RAY. We can't, Walter. You're not thinking. Phone and say what?

WALTER. Say what happened.

RAY. And who's going to believe that?

DEBORAH. I did.

RAY. That's because you know Richard. But everyone else will just jump on him. A girl raped, maybe killed, that must have been some sex freak. Sex freak equals retard. Retard equals Richard. Think about it.

DEBORAH. But still, you have to think about her.

RAY. No we don't.

DEBORAH. Well, we can't just leave her there to die.

RAY. There's nothing we can do, Deborah. We have to think about Richard. As far as I'm concerned Richard is the only part of this that matters.

DEBORAH. But Richard loves her, doesn't he?

RAY. That doesn't matter.

DEBORAH. I still think maybe we should phone somebody.

WALTER. We don't need the Police but we should get her an ambulance. We wouldn't have to say who we were.

RAY. I've already done that. I used a pay phone. I just told them where she was and that was all.

WALTER. What pay phone?

RAY. The one on the way home.

WALTER. What one?

RAY. What does it matter? The important thing is. None of this leaves this room. Do you hear me, Deborah?

DEBORAH. I don't know.

RAY. Well, let me put it like this. If you say something about this or do something that hurts our Richard, you can forget about becoming part of this family. Our Gordon won't want anything to do with you. Now, you're a nice girl and all that, and I hope the two of you's do work things out, but if it's between you and our Richard, Gordon'll pick him every time, I guarantee it.

DEBORAH. But . . .

RAY. There are no buts.

WALTER. What do you want me to do, Ray?

RAY. The same thing goes for you, Walter. You leave here and you don't know shit about it. You go and see whoever asked you to call over here and you tell them, we were all in bed sleeping and everything was honky-dory. Got it?

WALTER. No problem.

RAY. Don't try anything, Walter. You know the score with me.

WALTER. Nothing to fucking worry about here, mate. Nothing to worry about at all.

RAY. You tell Monroe about the other kids saying she left with the taig. Tell him that. And tell him that if he wants something done about it, I'm the man to do it. In fact I might just do it anyway. For Richard, you know.

WALTER. Ray, listen, I'm going to leave here and I'm going to tell nobody nothing. I think that's the best thing for it. Let them find out for themselves. I mean, I'll tell them about you's all being asleep and all, but I honestly think, that's all I should say about it.

RAY. Fair enough. I'll do the rest on my own.

DEBORAH. What are you going to do?

RAY. Deborah, listen, I just want to know that you're all right with this.

DEBORAH. What are you going to do?

RAY. That's not important. Forget about that. Think about this. You don't know nothing about tonight. You don't know nothing about a party, you don't know nothing about that wee girl. You just don't know nothing. Now, tell me what you know.

Silence.

WALTER. You're supposed to say, you don't know nothing.

RAY. Let me hear it from her, Walter. (*To* DEBORAH.) What do you know about this, Deborah?

DEBORAH. I don't know nothing.

RAY. Well done. Now, let's see what we can do about getting you home.

ACT THREE

Next morning.

WALTER *is sitting on the settee.* GORDON, *casually dressed, enters from the kitchen with two mugs of tea.* RAY, *partially dressed in the usual jeans and t-shirt, one boot on, enters from the hall.* WALTER *nods to him,* RAY *ignores* WALTER.

GORDON. Are you up?

RAY. I'm getting there. Where's Richard?

GORDON. He's out the back chopping sticks. If it gets any colder I'm going to have to light the fire.

RAY. It's not that cold.

GORDON. I'm not lighting it yet.

RAY. That's the first thing I'm going to do when you leave.

GORDON. What, light the fire?

RAY. Very funny. I'm going to get the oil in, go central heating and drag this place into the twentieth century.

GORDON. And how are you going to do that, when there won't be any money coming in?

RAY. You've just answered your own question.

GORDON. What are you talking about?

RAY. Whenever you go, we'll drop below the income support minimum or whatever the fuck you call it now, and that means we'll qualify for everything that's going.

WALTER. I don't think they do that caper any more, Ray.

RAY. Who says?

WALTER. It's all loans and all now.

GORDON. And you will never qualify for a loan, so there goes your central heating plan.

RAY. Is that right? Well we'll see what they say when I go down and tell them there is no heat and my Ma's upstairs dying of the cold, and our Richard's freezing to death.

GORDON. They won't say anything.

WALTER. They might give you money for coal or something.

RAY. And what if that fire doesn't work any more?

GORDON. They'll send an inspector out and he'll see there's nothing wrong with it.

RAY. Oh, yeah. What if I wreck the shite out of it before he gets here?

GORDON. Wise up, Ray.

RAY. Do you think it would work, Walter?

WALTER. It might.

RAY (*to* GORDON). Speaking of work, shouldn't you be somewhere else?

GORDON. I phoned in sick.

RAY. What for? You should be looking after that job.

WALTER. Work's hard to find. (*Takes a drink of tea.*)

GORDON. What would you's know about that now?

WALTER. Quite a lot actually. I worked in Shorts for fifteen years.

RAY. You must have been the only one.

WALTER. When I left it, I can tell you finding another job wasn't easy. Of course, because of my accident it would have been harder for me, but even for someone young and fit *and honest* like you I reckon it would still be hard these days.

GORDON. Good job I'm not looking for one then, isn't it?

RAY. Here, where's my tea?

GORDON. Take this. I'll get another cup.

RAY (*takes* GORDON*'s mug of tea off him and sits down at the table*). If you lost this job, you'd soon know all about it. You wouldn't be able to take your woman out for any more of those fancy dinners she likes. And you'd probably find your marriage being called off as well.

GORDON *goes into the kitchen.*

RAY. So, what's happening, Walter?

WALTER. I didn't want to say anything while Gordon was here. Is it OK to talk when he comes back in?

RAY. What's up?

WALTER. Things are going bad.

RAY. What way?

WALTER. Well, last night by the time I got back to the house I was told that Monroe was already down at the hospital and that Susan was in a really bad way. So, I headed straight down to the hospital myself.

RAY. Did you tell him we were all in bed when you came round?

WALTER. I never got a chance.

RAY. What do you mean?

WALTER. When I got there the man was fucking raging. I mean I've never seen him like that before. He was going on about how he wasn't being overly helpful with the Police.

GORDON *returns.*

GORDON. Why's that?

RAY. Gordon, is Deborah working today?

GORDON. No. (*To* WALTER.) Why would he not be helpful to the Police?

WALTER. He wants us to sort it for him. You can't really blame the man.

RAY. The Police would only protect the guy that did this.

WALTER. The problem is Susan was drifting in and out. I mean, she's in a really bad way. But Monroe says she spoke to him during the night.

GORDON. What did she say?

WALTER. She talked about Richard.

RAY. And what?

GORDON. It doesn't really surprise me that she would talk about our Richard. I mean they were at this party together. That could be the last thing she remembers.

WALTER. Maybe.

RAY. What did she say about him?

WALTER. Well, she only mumbled something about him. Monroe says he couldn't make it out too well.

GORDON. What does he think she said?

WALTER. She mentioned someone else.

RAY. Who?

WALTER. You're not going to like it.

RAY. Hurry up and tell us.

WALTER. You.

Silence.

RAY. And what about me?

WALTER. He could make a lot of noise about it.

RAY. Well he better be careful or he'll be spending a lot more time in hospital than just visiting.

WALTER. What am I suppose to tell everyone else.

RAY. Fuck everyone else.

WALTER. I think we have to come clean about what happened.

RAY. No, Walter.

WALTER. Well then, tell me what I'm supposed to say when he says, she said, one of you hurt her.

RAY. Who's he said this to?

WALTER. Only me. But he says if I don't get this sorted out, he'll be saying it to a lot more people.

GORDON. Why would she think one of you hurt her?

RAY. She's mixed up. It was the taig who hurt her. The wee girl's sick, she's been through a hectic fucking time, she's maybe getting things a bit confused, or else the Da is getting things deliberately confused, because let's face it there are a lot of people looking for an opportunity like this to get their knives out and try to cut me up. Well, it's not going to work. Let me tell you this. I don't care if she said my name. I mean I was there. It's not a big problem, apart from the fact that it pulls our Richard back into this again. But it's all right, I'll go and talk to him.

WALTER. So, do we come clean about what happened then?

RAY. You're going to have to go and speak to them, Walter.

GORDON. Who?

RAY. Walter knows who needs to know.

WALTER. What'll I say?

RAY. You tell them this. I want them to know that I saved that wee girl's life last night. Tell them about her and our Richard. Tell them everything, Walter.

WALTER. Yeah, but what about the bit about after you chased this guy off? Where did you go from there? I don't want to tell them that you left her there?

RAY. Not like that, no. You tell them I went straight to a phone box and then I had to get our Richard home. I didn't want him to see her and I was worried because I know what people are like. And I was right. First chance they get, what do they do? Blame him.

WALTER. So, what's the plan now?

RAY. Well, that's how you're going to wrap it up so nice for them.

WALTER. How?

RAY. Because you tell them, that I hope to be or you hope to be, whatever you like, but they're going to be given a good result within forty-eight hours.

WALTER. What result?

RAY. Celtic nil, Rangers one. Rangers take the championship and Celtic are relegated. Can you think of a better result than that?

GORDON. What does that mean, Ray?

RAY. That means I'm going to get the taig.

WALTER. Why didn't you get him at the time, I mean what am I supposed to say about that?

RAY. He was too far away.

GORDON. How far away was he?

RAY. Way, way down the bottom of the hill and running fast.

WALTER. Well, if he's way, way down a hill and running fast, how can you say it was definitely this guy?

RAY. Walter, she left the party with him.

WALTER. Hold on, thought you said last night that when you got there he was messing about with Richard and you beat him up and that's why after you left he attacked Susan.

RAY. That's right, that's how I know it was definitely him.

WALTER. Hold on a fucking minute, Ray.

RAY. What?

WALTER. You just said that when you got there he was way down the bottom of the hill.

RAY. That was the second time. The second time, when I went back because Richard wanted me to make sure Susan was all right.

WALTER. Right, fair enough.

RAY. Why, have you got some sort of fucking problem, Walter?

WALTER. No, no way, Ray. I just need to get everything sorted out so as no-one can say anything about us or Richard, know what I mean, mate?

RAY. And are you happy now?

WALTER. Oh, yeah. Except for just one other thing.

RAY. Go ahead, Colombo, what is it?

WALTER. What happens if this wee girl comes round and says something different from your story?

GORDON. Why would she do that, Walter?

WALTER. I'm just saying.

RAY. Walter's right to ask these questions, Gordon.

GORDON. I've no problem with asking questions, it's the way he's asking them.

WALTER. I don't mean anything by it, Gordon, mate. You know me, Ray. I just want to make sure we've got everything nailed down.

RAY. Well, here's the truth, Walter. That wee girl has been raped and beaten to within an inch of losing her life. When she comes round there is no telling what she might say or think. That's why, when I get this guy and make him confess, no-one will be asking her what happened or what she thinks happened. No, people will be telling her what really happened.

WALTER. Right.

GORDON. How are you going to get this confession?

RAY. You leave that to me.

WALTER. Can I just ask one more thing, Ray?

RAY. What?

WALTER. See when you did beat this guy up, why did you leave him there with Susan?

RAY. I just did.

WALTER. You just did.

RAY. Look, I was raging, alright. When I got there, he was making fun of our Richard, I lost my temper and I hurt him. All I wanted to do was get Richard home. But Richard wanted me to take her home as well but the wee fucker wouldn't come with us.

WALTER. Did you try to get her to come with you?

GORDON. Where's this going, Walter?

WALTER. It's not going anywhere. I just need to get everything straight in my head. Ray says he beat this guy up and then he tried to get her to come with him and Richard.

RAY. That's right.

WALTER. And then?

GORDON. And then what?

WALTER. That's what I'm asking.

RAY. And then she wouldn't come with us.

WALTER. And that was that?

RAY. That was that.

WALTER (*stands*). Ray, I'm talking to you now as your friend. Haven't I always seen you right?

RAY. What are you standing up for?

WALTER. I just want you to tell me the truth. I need to know the truth. I don't care what it is, I just need to know it.

RAY. Sit down.

WALTER. Did Richard attack this wee girl?

GORDON. You better sit down, Walter.

RAY. Don't make me get up and knock you down.

WALTER. I know he didn't deliberately attack her, but things can happen. All I'm saying is, talk to me. Just . . . Did something happen? Did Richard hurt this wee girl – by accident?

RAY. If you ask me that one more time, I'll knock your cunt in.

WALTER. If he did. Gordon? (*Pause.*) If he did maybe we can work something out.

RAY. Like what? Which lamp-post to hang him from after we've shot his nuts off?

WALTER. There would be no need for that.

RAY. Yes there would. And if our Richard had have attacked that wee girl, I would be the first in line to do it, but he didn't.

WALTER. But things happen, Ray. Things that can be explained.

GORDON. Our Richard would never have hurt Susan. There's just no way he could do it.

RAY. This girl was nearly beaten to death, Walter. I seen her. And I can tell you our Richard could not have fucking done that.

WALTER. But you could've.

RAY. What?

WALTER. Now don't be getting fucking out of hand here, Ray.

GORDON. You're the one that's getting out of hand, Walter.

WALTER. Hear me out. Things can happen, you know what I'm saying, maybe when you got there Richard was having sex with this girl.

GORDON. No, no.

WALTER. Maybe he raped her.

RAY. Walter!

WALTER. And maybe she said she was going to tell on him and you had to keep her quiet. So you tried to talk to her and when that didn't work you started beating her.

GORDON. I can't believe you're standing there accusing Ray of doing this.

WALTER. I'm not accusing anybody of anything. All I'm saying Ray, is if something like that happened we can work something out. You know, but if you're lying to me, then I can't help you.

RAY. I'm not lying to you when I tell you this, Walter. If you ever say anything like that about any member of my family ever again, I'll beat you to death.

WALTER. Well, OK. But listen, I think it would be a good idea to get Richard out of this, away from here quickly, before things get out of hand.

RAY. Listen Walter. If anyone's going to get out of hand, you tell them to come and see me.

WALTER. I don't think you realise how serious this is.

RAY. You've got other problems and so do we, Walter. I suggest you do what you have to do and you let me get on with doing what I have to do.

WALTER. All I'm going to do is carry the information. You do what you like.

RAY. You'll have to explain to Monroe what happened. Tell him he can come with me and get his own revenge if he wants to.

WALTER. No. You do it yourself, as yourself.

GORDON. Hold on, Ray.

RAY. Walter. (*Pause.*) I'm going to need one of those video cameras and tapes and all. Send Dougie with them. He knows how they work.

WALTER. Where are you going to do all this?

RAY. Leave that to me.

WALTER. I can get you keys to a flat. It's been empty for months. You know the one I mean, big Ronnie's supposed to be living there, that's what the dole think anyway.

RAY. That'll do. And don't worry, it'll be clean.

RAY *walks towards the kitchen.*

GORDON. Where are you going?

RAY. I'm going to see Richard. Listen, you're going to be staying in all day, aren't you?

GORDON. I don't know.

RAY. Well can you make a decision? I don't want Richard left on his own.

GORDON. OK. I'll stay in.

RAY. Get Deborah to come over if you like.

Exit RAY.

GORDON. Have you to get going then, Walter?

WALTER. Things are getting out of hand, Gordon. (*Pause.*)

GORDON. What do you mean?

WALTER. You're the one that it all comes down to.

GORDON. What are you talking about?

WALTER. He could kill this guy. (*Pause.*) He might have to.

GORDON. He won't kill him. So long as Susan isn't dead, there's no need for anyone else to be dead, isn't that the way it works? You heard him, he's just going to get him to confess.

WALTER. You're a Christian, aren't you?

GORDON. So what?

WALTER. So does that seem all right to you? Your brother's going to make someone confess to a crime that no-one can prove he committed. And no-one's going to believe he committed either. Think about it, Gordon. He's doing this to clear Richard, but he's only going to create more problems than he's going to solve. If this wee girl gets better, whatever she says is what people are going to believe and at the minute it looks like she's going to be pointing the finger at at least one member of your family.

GORDON. What are you telling me this for?

WALTER. You could do something about it.

GORDON. Get to the crunch, Walter.

RAY *brings* RICHARD *into the living room.*

WALTER. Think about it.

RAY. Listen to this, Walter.

WALTER. I'm listening.

RAY. Do you swear to tell the truth, the whole truth and nothing but the truth, so help you God?

RICHARD. Yes.

RAY. Where were you on the night in question?

RICHARD. I was at a party and afterwards I went up the Hill because Susan had gone up the Hill with some fella.

RAY. And this guy was doing things to Susan when you got there.

RICHARD. Yes.

RAY. Who was this guy?

RICHARD. His name is Michael and he's a Catholic.

RAY. How's that?

GORDON. Is that the truth, Richard?

RAY. Wasn't he under oath?

RICHARD. Can I go and see Susan now?

RAY. What did I tell you?

WALTER. I don't think that would be a good idea at the moment, son.

RAY. Tomorrow.

RICHARD. Are you going to talk to her Da for me, Ray?

GORDON. Maybe it would be better if you waited for a few days.

RICHARD. But I want to see her.

RAY. We'll sort something out for you, our kid. I have to go here, Gordon.

RAY *walks towards door leading to hall.*

GORDON. Where are you for now?

RAY. Things to do, bro'. See you later. (*Pause.*) Walter, video stuff, Dougie with the keys, at the flat. Give me an hour and a half.

WALTER. No problem.

Exit RAY.

RICHARD. Do you want to see a card trick? It's a weaser. Take a card, any card as long as it's a ten or under a ten.

WALTER *looks at* GORDON *before taking a card.*

RICHARD. How many times do you think I would have to go through this deck, quickly like, before I'd know what your card is?

WALTER. What do you reckon, Gordon?

GORDON. I don't think he can do it.

RICHARD. I won't even go through the deck twice. Are you ready?

WALTER. Do you understand what's happening with Susan, Richard? (RICHARD *shakes his head because he is trying to concentrate on counting the cards.*) If Gordon was to leave here and live somewhere else, would you go with him?

GORDON. I've already asked him to do that, he turned us down.

WALTER. What if it was somewhere good?

RICHARD. Hold on! Hold on! (*Closes his eyes tight, then begins to go through the deck again.*)

GORDON. Deborah and I have a house, Walter. He's not interested. He wants to stay with Ray.

WALTER. What if Ray had to go away somewhere?

RICHARD. Three of diamonds.

WALTER. Correct. (*Doesn't look at the card, but returns it to* RICHARD.)

RICHARD. Ray taught me that one.

WALTER. What do you think?

RICHARD. I think I have to show this one to Susan tomorrow.

WALTER. Maybe you shouldn't go and see Susan.

RICHARD. Why not?

WALTER. Because of what happened.

GORDON. Maybe you should forget about Susan, Richard.

RICHARD. No way. You wouldn't forget about Deborah if I asked you to.

GORDON. What if I did?

RICHARD. No. No deal. No way. You've already fallen out with Deborah, probably. Me and Susan are going to get back together. You're just trying to trick me.

GORDON. I haven't fallen out with Deborah.

RICHARD. Doesn't matter. Deborah would be easy to forget.

GORDON. Richard?

RICHARD. Do you want to see another trick?

WALTER. I seen Susan today.

RICHARD. Did you? Did he Gordon?

WALTER. Do you know what she said?

RICHARD. Did she ask about me?

WALTER. She said Ray hurt her.

Silence.

RICHARD *shrugs.*

WALTER. Why would she say that?

RICHARD. I don't know.

WALTER. Did Ray hurt her?

RICHARD. No, it was the fenian that hurt her.

GORDON. Did Ray tell you to say that?

RICHARD. It wasn't Ray. It was the fenian.

WALTER. That's not true. She says it was Ray. So either she's a liar or Ray is.

RICHARD. Why don't you ask Ray if he's a liar when he comes back, Walter?

GORDON. Richard, we're in trouble here. Ray's going to do something terrible. Tell me what really happened.

WALTER. Is your girlfriend a lying little slut?

RICHARD. What?

WALTER. Susan. Ray says she's a lying little slut. Do you think she is?

GORDON. Walter?

WALTER. She must be, she's trying to say your brother hurt her. Why would she say that? She mustn't like your family. She must be a dirty lying wee slut, bitch.

RICHARD. I'm going to tell Ray what you said.

WALTER. Ray'll tell you himself. That's what he told us.

RICHARD. No he said he wouldn't tell anybody.

WALTER. He told us.

RICHARD. And anyway she's not a slut anymore.

WALTER. Ray said she was.

RICHARD. But Ray said he sorted her out for me. She won't be a slut no more.

GORDON. Wait, wait, wait! Hold on here.

RICHARD. You're going to get sorted out too, Walter. I don't like you no more.

GORDON. How did Ray sort her out for you?

RICHARD. He just did.

GORDON. This is very important, Richard. How did he sort her out?

WALTER. Did Ray hurt her?

RICHARD (*walks to the table*). I'm not talking to you any more.

GORDON (*joins* RICHARD *at the table*). What happened?

RICHARD. Do you want a game?

GORDON. Deal me in.

RICHARD (*deals*). I thought Christians didn't play cards.

GORDON. What happened, Richard?

RICHARD. I want to see Susan, Gordon.

GORDON. There's a lot of people wouldn't like that, mate.

RICHARD. I have to talk to her. Ray's got it wrong. She's not . . . (*Sighs.*) Well . . . (*Shrugs, saddened. Struggles to talk.*) I just need to tell her something.

GORDON. Tell me.

RICHARD. He won't do it again. It's sorted. She just has to realise what the score is. We'll go for a walk up the hill again. Maybe a different hill. We'll just talk for ages, well, she will. I'll listen, I love listening to her talking. She's got a lovely voice. Not many people notice that, but she has. And she's got lovely hands too. They're warm and wet. I tried to tell her that this fella shouldn't be doing that kind of thing to her. But he just called me names and cracked jokes about me. Ray was raging and the taig got scared and ran away. I didn't hear him acting big and calling our Ray names, no, he just ran away as fast as he could.

WALTER. He ran away . . .

GORDON *indicates that* WALTER *should let* RICHARD *finish his story. He does so.*

RICHARD. Then Ray wanted me to get home, but I waited, because I wanted him to make sure Susan got home. Susan was in bad form, Ray says that's what happens when wee girls drink. I could hear shouting and screaming. He started calling her names, she called him names too. You shouldn't really do that, like. He slapped her, hard in the face. (*Pauses, disgusted, confused.*) She said she would get her Da for him. Ray said what he would do to her Da and the names she called him was wild.

GORDON. What did he do?

RICHARD. He said he had to talk to her. And that he would sort her out for me. I shouldn't have left her alone with him. I ran away, I didn't know what to do. I was going to come home, but sure . . . I think she liked Ray better than me.

GORDON. Why? What do you mean by that?

RICHARD. They were doing it. I seen them. I can't do that. She . . . can.

GORDON. That's all right, don't think about it anymore.

RICHARD. Ray stopped. She kept calling him names. And then when he saw me he lost it. He gave her a real digging. That shut her up. I didn't know what to do. Ray says not to worry, we'd send an ambulance. See, I didn't know she was a slut. But Ray says she won't be no more. And if she ever is, I've just to tell him and he'll sort her out for me. But I wouldn't tell him. Because I think he really hurt her. And I . . . (*Stops.*)

WALTER. Gordon!

RICHARD. You won't tell Ray I told you, sure you won't?

GORDON. Richard, go up and stay with my Mum for two seconds.

RICHARD *turns the cards over.*

RICHARD. I won.

RICHARD *leaves the room.*

WALTER. You're going to have to think your options, Gordon. What's the most important thing here?

GORDON. Walter, give me a minute, will you?

WALTER. There's no time. Are you listening to me? We've got two stories here and when Susan comes around we'll probably have a third story. If we were to ask the taig maybe a fourth. Now, if we do nothing Ray will probably kill this guy. Do you want to let that happen?

GORDON. Of course I don't.

WALTER. Then there's Richard.

GORDON. We can't ever let anybody hear what Richard told us, Walter.

WALTER. I agree with you. I know what would happen if we tell them Ray did it. You'd have to turn him over to the Police

or I'd have to turn him over to Monroe and start a whole
internal feud. No, forget about that.

GORDON. So, what do we do?

WALTER. Why don't you go to the Police?

GORDON. And what?

WALTER. They would protect Richard.

GORDON. Richard! What does Richard need to be protected
for?

WALTER. I'm just saying.

GORDON. You're just saying what?

WALTER. OK. I think no matter what happens. No matter who
says what. People will never believe that it wasn't Richard
who did this. (*Speeds up.*) In situations like this. It isn't
always a case of what really should be done, it's more a case
of what most people think should be done. Do you see what
I'm saying? If we say Ray did it. First of all, Ray won't hand
himself over. Secondly, it would be too easy to make a case
out for him. As he said himself, a lot of people are out to get
him. Or, as well as that, most people would think he was only
being a hero trying to protect his wee brother. They'll still
come after Richard. Why should two of your brothers be
punished? And in trying to get to Richard, who else might get
hurt. You have other people to think about. Not least of all
your pretty girlfriend. Ever heard of an eye for an eye? And
what about your Ma?

GORDON. My Ma has nothing to do with this. Neither has
Deborah.

WALTER. Come on, Gordon. Be realistic.

GORDON. I am not handing my innocent brother over to the
Police to ruin his life, just because it's what most people
think should be done.

WALTER. It wouldn't necessarily ruin his life.

GORDON. Of course it would.

WALTER. OK. Then, there's one other option.

GORDON. Which is?

WALTER. Do him.

GORDON. Do him?

WALTER. One shot in the knee. You don't have to hit the bone.

GORDON (*interrupts*) Don't!

WALTER. Think about it. If you don't do it, Monroe might get someone else to do it. And how do you know they'll do it right? One thing you can't deny, Gordon. Somebody is going to have to do something. This isn't going to blow away. No matter what Ray does, it won't count, when the finger is pointed at this family, somebody, some new kid on the block, some pup that wants to make a name for himself, taking on Ray, or just doing a favour for Monroe. You bet your fucking arse, somebody will step out of a crowd and somebody else will put a gun in that boy's hand, and who knows what kind of shit will happen? Now, you, you have the options, right here and right now. But they just ran out. You won't go to the Police, you won't move away and you know you can't take Ray on. So what? Tell me, honestly, what! What are you going to do?

Silence

What I'm talking about here, Gordon. Is a little nick. Not a bullet in the head or a shattered knee cap. A little nick, a tiny little scratch. Know what I'm saying? It's all superficial but it'll carry the weight, 'cause it's not about the wound, it's about the act and it's about the will to carry out the act, that's remorse and that's respect. This act will be a tremendous piece of courage and this act, believe me, will be an act a man like Monroe will have to respect. And above all the bullshit, above everything, let me just say this. It's not too late – no-one's dead yet. If you were to do this. If you were to do it soon. That would be it finished for ever.

GORDON (*hesitates*). How would I know that for sure? What guarantees would I have?

WALTER. I can give you my word that you's will be left alone.

GORDON. I was hoping for a bit more than that, Walter.

WALTER. We're running out of time.

GORDON. I don't even have a gun.

WALTER *places a gun on the table in front of* GORDON.

ACT FOUR

Living room, later.

GORDON. I don't know why I brought you over here, Deborah. I don't know whether I want you to talk me into something or talk me out of something.

DEBORAH. What is it that you think you have to do?

GORDON. I don't know, but I just . . . I just feel as if I need to talk to someone.

DEBORAH. Talk to God.

GORDON. God has nothing to do with it. I was thinking of going to the Police, but I don't know what would happen.

DEBORAH. No you can't. I think we should pray.

GORDON. No! I can't do it, it doesn't work. I need help.

DEBORAH. But no-one can help us, especially not the Police. That's why we have to trust in the Lord, Gordon.

GORDON. Why, what's he going to do? (*Pause.*) Is he going to make my Ma better. She can't even get out of her bed any more. What's he going to do about Richard? Is he going to take him away from here, make this all go away. And what about Ray?

DEBORAH. Ask him.

GORDON. I don't want to ask him.

DEBORAH. Why not?

GORDON. Because. Because I don't want to hear what he wants.

DEBORAH. Ask God what he wants for us, Gordon?

GORDON. What do you mean?

DEBORAH. All I've heard out of you is about your Mum, Richard or Ray, always someone else, Gordon. Maybe all these things are a sign. Maybe all these problems are his way of telling us that we don't belong here. The Lord works in mysterious ways.

GORDON. Talk to me in English, not Hebrew.

DEBORAH. Listen to your heart. Richard is an example. What if we have our own kids? Would you want them mixed up with their Uncle Ray? Would you, Gordon? No, you'd maybe want the odd visit, just to keep in touch, but would you want the visit to be in some prison somewhere? Or a graveyard?

GORDON. Of course I wouldn't.

DEBORAH. Well then?

GORDON. Well then, what?

DEBORAH. Let God sort it out. There's nothing you can do.

GORDON. There's plenty I can do.

DEBORAH. Like what?

GORDON. I could go to the Police and they could get Ray.

DEBORAH. You can't. You wouldn't be able to live with yourself, Gordon. And think about it, what about your Mum. Who would look after her? What about Richard?

GORDON. I could sort something out.

DEBORAH. You couldn't Gordon. Your family wouldn't want you any more. Your Mum would end up in a home. She'd die there. She doesn't want that, you know she doesn't. And Richard, some crazy place full of really sick people. What would happen to him there? He would just get sicker and sicker.

GORDON. We could look after them.

DEBORAH. We couldn't. They wouldn't let us. And even . . . Even if they did, we'd be waiting on Ray getting out. And they . . . Your Mum would never forgive you. Never.

GORDON. She wouldn't know.

DEBORAH. I would know. And I'd be waiting for him every night, every waking hour.

GORDON. Deborah!

DEBORAH. This is a sign, Gordon. What Ray does, what happens, that's in God's hands, leave it there.

GORDON. I can't.

DEBORAH. Look, it might be for the best. If . . . (*Making it up as she goes along.*) If you weren't here. Ray, would have to look after your Mum and Richard by himself. He wouldn't have any more time to get in to trouble or do whatever it is you don't want him to do any more. (*Pause.*) All I'm saying is, Gordon, listen to God.

GORDON. I can't hear God.

DEBORAH. Then listen harder. Because if I'm the only one that can hear him, then that might mean that I'm the only one he wants to leave.

GORDON. What if I could hear God? What if I knew exactly what he wanted me to do, but I didn't want to do it?

DEBORAH. You have to do it.

GORDON. So you're saying that if a person thinks God is wrong he should just go ahead and do what he's told.

DEBORAH. I'm not sure I understand what you mean, Gordon.

GORDON. God asked Abraham.

DEBORAH. We've been through this before.

GORDON. But you said he wouldn't ask me, Deborah. But I'm saying he has asked me.

DEBORAH. What is it that you're saying God has asked you to do?

GORDON. He's asked me to shoot my own brother.

DEBORAH. What?

GORDON (*goes and gets gun*). And he gave me this.

DEBORAH. Where did you get that? Is it Ray's?

GORDON. Walter gave me it.

DEBORAH. What for?

GORDON. He said that no-one is going to believe us. He said that Susan is pointing the finger at this family. It could be Ray or it could be Richard. But most people think it's got to be Richard. Most people wouldn't have the guts to take Ray on anyway. So, that's how you know it's going to be Richard.

DEBORAH. But Richard hasn't done anything.

GORDON. Do you think I don't know that?

DEBORAH. Why don't we ring one of the Pastors? One of the young ones that you like. They can handle things like this and it would be confidential.

GORDON. You don't get it, Deborah.

DEBORAH. Get what?

GORDON. If I believe, if I trust God, then I will be sort of taking Richard up to the hill, but if I really believe then God will not let me go through with it, know what I mean? God will provide something else.

DEBORAH. I don't think you're thinking about this properly, Gordon. What has Walter been saying?

GORDON. Forget about Walter. Walter is not the problem, I am. I am the problem, do you know why? I don't believe. I really don't believe.

DEBORAH. Look Gordon, you've been through a lot recently. A lot of things have happened. The first thing we have to do is get rid of the gun.

GORDON. But if I'm supposed to do what God says, then I'm going to need this gun.

DEBORAH. You don't need the gun, Gordon. You need to think about what you're doing.

GORDON. What am I doing?

DEBORAH. You're acting like a crazy person. God doesn't want you to shoot Richard.

GORDON. Everybody wants me to shoot Richard. Do you know what's going to happen if I don't shoot Richard?

DEBORAH. Gordon, nobody is going to shoot Richard.

GORDON. Oh, yes they are. But they're honourable men and they are giving me the opportunity to do it first. Like a family thing. But if I don't do it, then they're going to come after us and they might hurt all of us. Me, my Mum and you. And to stop all this all I have to do, is do it myself.

We hear the back door opening and various noises as RAY *crashes through the kitchen into the living room. He has been shot in the stomach. He is exhausted and in a terrible state. He slumps to the ground.*

RAY. Deep fucking shit, mate. Deep fucking shit.

GORDON. What has happened? Ray, what the hell's happened to you?

RAY. I'm in big trouble, mate. Things have gotten out of hand.

DEBORAH. You'll have to phone an ambulance.

RAY. No! No phones.

GORDON. Deborah's right, Ray. Look at you. You need help.

RAY. Forget about that.

GORDON. What are you going to do?

RAY. I want to see my Ma.

> RAY *attempts to make it to the stairs but gives up and leans against the wall to rest.*

GORDON. Ray, let me help you please.

DEBORAH. You need help, Ray.

RAY. There is no help. They'll be here soon.

GORDON. Who?

RAY. The bastards.

DEBORAH. Gordon, you'll have to do something.

RAY. Where's Richard?

GORDON. He's upstairs. What's going on?

RAY. The bitch died.

GORDON. What?

RAY. She just fucking died and obviously she's just lived long enough to point a huge fucking finger at us.

GORDON. Ray!

RAY. They came for me straight away. Walter set me up. Bastard!

GORDON. We've got to get the Police, Ray.

RAY. No! Fuck that.

GORDON. We have to get somebody.

RAY. Listen to me, Gordon. It's all down to you, mate.

GORDON. What'll I do?

RAY. Where'd you get the gun?

GORDON. Walter.

RAY. Obviously.

GORDON. He said if I just nicked our Richard in the leg, it would be enough.

RAY. What a cunt.

GORDON. I wasn't going to do it.

RAY. Well, it wouldn't matter now, anyway.

DEBORAH. Gordon, get on the phone.

Enter RICHARD.

RICHARD. What's going on? (*Notices* RAY.) Ray! What's happening?

RAY. Nothing, son. Go back up to my Ma.

RICHARD. What are you doing?

RAY. Do what you're told for once in your fucking life.

RICHARD. No.

RAY. Deborah. Me and Gordon have to sort this out. Take him up, will you?

RICHARD. No.

DEBORAH. Gordon?

GORDON. Do it, Deborah.

DEBORAH. I can't. I'm not leaving you here, with that.

RAY. Get her out of here, Gordon, come on, mate. We don't have time for bullshit.

GORDON. Go Deborah, don't worry. We'll sort this out.

DEBORAH. How?

GORDON. Deborah! Deborah, do it.

RAY. Go with Deborah, Richard.

RICHARD. No.

RAY. Let me see the gun, Gordon.

DEBORAH. Don't do it, Gordon.

GORDON. Whatever it is, you're thinking about, Ray. It won't work. I'm not going to do it.

RAY. You have to mate.

GORDON. No, I don't.

RAY. Listen, word's out. They're coming after us.

RICHARD. Well, we can fucking do them when they get here. Gordon's got a gun.

GORDON. Shut up, Richard.

RICHARD. Why not?

RAY. Come here, Richard. Come on, come here.

RICHARD. What?

RAY. I have to tell you something.

RICHARD. What is it?

GORDON. Ray, let me talk to him later. We've no time now.

RAY. There's time for this.

RICHARD. What is it?

RAY. You know I love you mate, don't you?

RICHARD. What is it?

RAY. It's about Susan.

RICHARD. What about her? Here, you could end up in the
    same hospital and I could come and visit the both of you at
    the same time.

RAY. You can't.

DEBORAH. Gordon –

GORDON. Wait!

RICHARD. Gordon'll take me.

RAY. There's no nice way to tell you this, mate.

RICHARD. Then just tell me.

RAY. Susan died this morning. I'm really fucking sorry, mate.

RICHARD. Why?

RAY. Come here.

They hug. WALTER *is at the front door.*

DEBORAH. Is that them?

RAY. What do you want to bet me, that's Walter?

GORDON. What'll I do?

RAY. Let the cunt in.

RICHARD. It's probably his fault.

RAY. What?

RICHARD. Walter. He said you called her a slut and a lying wee
    bitch and all that. You said you wouldn't tell anyone.

RAY. Richard! Richard, listen to me.

RICHARD. Why don't we do him?

RAY. Listen! Deborah's here as proof. You say if I tell a lie, Deborah.

DEBORAH. Right.

RAY. Are you listening?

RICHARD. Go.

RAY. You know the way, you and Susan are meant to always be together?

RICHARD. We can't now.

RAY. I know you can't. But that's because of her and the taig fella. God seen all that, and God told me that he would have to take Susan away to make her better.

RICHARD. Up in heaven.

RAY. Yeah.

RICHARD. Is that true?

DEBORAH. Yes.

RAY. Now, just to make sure everything's all right, the way it should be, I'm going to have to go and look after her. Do you know what I mean?

RICHARD. Why can't I go instead?

RAY. Because you have to stay here and look after my Ma and Gordon.

RICHARD. I don't want to.

RAY. You have to mate.

Enter GORDON *and* WALTER.

RICHARD. It's all his fucking fault.

WALTER. Ray. What happened, mate?

RAY. As if you don't know.

WALTER. Hey! I'm here to try and help you out of this, mate.

RAY. You're here to help yourself, cuntie and don't try to make it out any other way.

WALTER. Listen.

RAY. No, you listen. I know who's out there, and I know why they've sent you in. Thing is, Walter, I'm not going.

WALTER. You should think about it, Ray.

RAY. What do you think I'm thinking about?

WALTER. Gordon! If he doesn't come out with me, they'll come in and get him.

GORDON. Walter's right, Ray. What are we going to do?

DEBORAH. We have to phone the police.

RAY (*struggles to his feet*). It's all down to you, Gordon, mate.

GORDON. What is? What are you talking about?

WALTER. Give me the gun, Gordon.

RAY. Give him fuck all.

GORDON. What are you thinking of?

RAY. I've come back here to make my peace with Richard. I've done it. Have I not?

RICHARD. What do you mean?

RAY. Are we friends?

RICHARD. Yes. But I don't want you to go.

RAY. Remember what I said.

DEBORAH. What are we going to do, Gordon?

WALTER. Give me the gun, mate.

GORDON. Shut up, Walter.

RAY. I've made my peace, Gordon. And I've asked God to forgive me, so it's all down to you mate.

GORDON. Fuck this!

RAY. Listen to me! I'm fucked. I'm not going to prison and I'm not going to spend the rest of my life in a fucking wheelchair as a fucking vegetable. It's up to you, Gordon. You have to be the man.

GORDON. Fuck it, I'm phoning the Police.

RAY. Look at me. I did it. I held her down, I spread her legs and I fucked her, Gordon. Look at me! Look at me! I fucked her and then I beat her Gordon. I beat her to death. She demands justice. Now I'm asking you as your brother. Do me before I start sinning all over again.

GORDON *holds the gun to* RAY's *head.*

GORDON. Fuck you!

DEBORAH. No Gordon!

RAY. Come on! Be a man for once in your fucking life.

GORDON. I can't fucking do it, Ray. Will you get that into your fucking head?

RICHARD. Why don't we bust out, Ray?

DEBORAH *makes her way by* RAY *to the phone.*

DEBORAH. I'm going to phone the Police.

WALTER. Big mistake.

WALTER *swipes at* DEBORAH. GORDON *wrestles with* WALTER. GORDON *drops the gun.*

DEBORAH. Gordon!

RICHARD *picks up the gun.*

RICHARD. Stop it!

RAY. Do me, wee man, do me. Do me now!

GORDON. Wait.

RAY *slaps* RICHARD, *hard.* RICHARD *shoots* RAY.

GORDON. No.

DEBORAH. Oh, my God.

GORDON. No. No.

RICHARD *drops the gun and hugs* RAY. RAY *is sitting dying.*

RICHARD. I'm sorry, Ray.

RAY. You're the man. You're the fucking man.

The End.

TEARING THE LOOM

Thanks to Sandra and Chuck Mitchell
– my Mum, Dad and family –
Joe Devlin, Robin Midgely
and David Grant.

And special thanks to Carol.

Tearing the Loom was commissioned
by the Lyric Theatre with the support
of the National Lottery through
the Arts Council of Northern Ireland

Tearing the Loom was first performed at the Lyric Theatre, Belfast, on 17 March 1998 with the following cast:

THE HAMILLS

SAMUEL, *the Grand Master* Frank O'Sullivan
WILLIAM, *his son* Ruairi Conaghan

THE MOORES

ROBERT, *a master weaver* Luke Hayden
DAVID, *his son* Miceal McBrian
ANNE, *his mother* Barbara Adair
RUTH, *his daughter* Diane O'Kelly

THE UNITED IRISHMAN

HARRY Tom Maguire

Director David Grant
Set and Costume Designer Gary McCann
Lighting Designer Wallace McDowell
Music Neil Martin
Deputy Stage Manager Rachel Foy Smith

The play is set near Tandragee, Co Armagh, in 1798.

PROLOGUE

The sound of the invisible loom establishes the atmosphere.
SAMUEL *stands centre stage, armed with two pistols and a sword. His clothes are bloodied.* WILLIAM, *his son, stands next to him. On the ground beside them lies a woman and a rope. Her head is covered and her hands are tied behind her back. She is crying, begging to be released and for the hood to be removed to enable her to see. Neither wish is granted.*

WILLIAM. Who is this?

SAMUEL. You don't need to know that, William. What you do need to know is that I found her hiding in a ditch with her husband.

WILLIAM. Why is she alone now?

SAMUEL. He was dead.

WILLIAM. Is she a Catholic?

SAMUEL. Most assuredly Catholic because of her prayers.

WILLIAM. Are we going to get information from her?

SAMUEL. She has nothing to give us.

WILLIAM. Then, what are we going to do with her?

SAMUEL. *We're* not going to do anything with her, William.

WILLIAM. I don't understand.

   SAMUEL *picks the rope up and ties it to a stick.*

WILLIAM. Father! The day's been long, if this woman's of no use to us, why are wasting our time when we could be resting?

SAMUEL. She has her purpose. A Presbyterian traitor would've been better but she'll do.

   SAMUEL *paces up and down before returning to his spot. There is a still silence as* WILLIAM *watches him put the finishing touches to the garrotte.*

WILLIAM. Father!

   The woman continues to mumble.

WILLIAM. What now?

SAMUEL. William, young as you are, I know today has been as
long as the blood has been deep. But listen to me, this day's
work is not done. Today you have failed in both your duty to
me and your duty to God!

WILLIAM. I've said I'm sorry.

SAMUEL. There is no need for apologies. Many have failed
since the rumours of this rebellion began. But stay your
failure. Grasp this nettle and prove yourself worthy to
become a true son of God. Remember your scriptures.
Proverbs 20 and 18. Every purpose is established by counsel
and with good advice make war. This rebellion is a war
against God and you and I alike have been wrought from soil
and clay and fashioned into warriors that we may protect the
children of God from their enemies.

WILLIAM. But Father she . . .

SAMUEL (*interrupts*). This – death – is the final weapon to be
used only against the enemies of God. Put her hair away if
you will and see not her bosom unless you are prepared to
look deep within and see for yourself the devil that beats in
her heart. For shall not the devil choose to show himself in
the very form which your heart considers to be beautiful and
desires with every beat to hold and to make your own? This
wretch and many like her, see them with true eyes. Our land,
our honour and our heritage and indeed all our worldly
possessions and no doubt our heavenly mansions are the very
items her soul craves to steal from us. Be not witness to her
shape or her form. Smell her wickedness as you place the
rope around her neck.

WILLIAM. Where's she to stand?

SAMUEL. Just place the rope around her neck. Don't permit her
to confound you with her muttering. You think you hear
pleading and begging, but what she utters are spells to damn
us all to hell. The rope William.

WILLIAM *has some difficulty lifting the woman to her feet.*

WILLIAM. She can't stand.

SAMUEL. I know! I had to prevent her from escaping.

WILLIAM *holds her while* SAMUEL *places the rope around
her neck. Then as* SAMUEL *takes hold of the woman*
WILLIAM *steps back.*

SAMUEL. Remember all the children that she slaughtered from Wexford to Down. Hear their cries and think of their mothers, poor heavenly creatures, not like this demon from hell. On my command twist the rope hard and the snap will send her straight back to that pit. Do it for God and do it for Ireland. Resist the feelings that many righteous men have felt before you. Indulge me and make of this wretch an example to all the demons from hell.

WILLIAM *holds the stick but doesn't twist.*

SAMUEL. William! You have let yourself and your name down once today already, do not do it again. For I know that in your chest beats a heart of solid gold. But I will run this steel through you if you hesitate when I command you next to do God's will.

WILLIAM (*unconvincing*). I hear you.

SAMUEL. Today we have shot and hanged many enemies of God and the King and tomorrow we will seize the opportunity to add to our total in honour of our oath:

In the awful presence of Almighty God . . .

WILLIAM *joins him in reciting the oath.*

I do solemnly swear that I will to the utmost of my power, support the King and present Government; and I do further swear that I will use my utmost exertions to exterminate all the Catholics of the kingdom of Ireland.

Pause.

SAMUEL. Do it!

WILLIAM *twists hard on the rope and the woman is killed. After a pause* SAMUEL *passes a drink to* WILLIAM *who has let go of the stick and stepped aside. He takes a drink, smiles – almost breaks down – then hugs his father.*

SAMUEL. Good man. Good man.

WILLIAM *sobs, then smiles.*

WILLIAM. I did it.

WILLIAM *gulps the drink down.*

SAMUEL. Let's go home.

The sound of the working loom becomes louder and more frenetic as the lights go down.

ACT ONE

ROBERT *sits at the loom.* DAVID *sits near him.* DAVID *is restless but pretends he is paying attention.* ROBERT *signals to* DAVID *who sighs as he lowers his head.*

ROBERT. Let's hear it again, David.

Pause.

DAVID. How many times do I have to go over and over the same thing?

ROBERT. You tell me.

ANNE *enters and* ROBERT *stops working and leans on the loom.*

ANNE. I've made you some tea. Are you going to come in and get it or do you want a tired old woman to carry it all the way in here?

ROBERT. Listen to this and we'll come in with you.

DAVID. I'll go and get it.

ROBERT. Once we've heard you, we can all get our tea.

ANNE. Do you not remember it, David?

ROBERT. Of course he remembers it, we've spent months going over and over it.

DAVID. Seems like years.

ROBERT. David do it!

ANNE. Have you not learned your lesson, Robert? With the youngster's heart pulling him to be somewhere else, his head empties of everything you try to put into it.

ROBERT. You make a fine woman of our Ruth and leave young David here to me.

ANNE. What's her name, David?

DAVID. Whose name?

ANNE. This girl, is there only one or have you them spread all over?

ROBERT. Mother, this is important. Let him do it and then we'll stop for tea. Come on David. Stand up there and tell it all back to me.

DAVID *shrugs.*

ANNE. Your father had quite a few girls before your mother captured him. Lord knows he's had none since she passed away. Those joys belong to you now.

DAVID. I don't know what you're talking about.

ROBERT. Mother, this can wait!

ANNE. Girls. Tell me which one is waiting out there.

ROBERT. I'm trying to teach him something of importance here.

ANNE. Teach him manners then, by showing him an example. Like respect for an old woman.

ROBERT. Son, do you want to learn with me or do you want to waste your time with idle chat about girls?

ANNE. All I want is a name to put to it.

DAVID. I don't know what she's talking about.

ANNE. If you were teaching him how to chase the girls you would get more attention from him, Robert.

ROBERT. If he listens to me and works hard he will not need to chase girls. They will come running from all over to chase him.

ANNE. What's her name David?

DAVID. There is no girl.

ROBERT (*to* DAVID). Maybe you could do a little work.

ROBERT *moves away from the loom offering his space to* DAVID.

ANNE. What is it that prevents you from learning?

DAVID. Nothing.

ROBERT. Come on, David. Work the loom then you can talk us through it.

ANNE. He looks very tired.

ROBERT. Who would work the loom tomorrow if I was suddenly taken ill?

ANNE. What illness could affect you? You're as hungry for life as you were the day I brought you into this world and from then until now how many complaints of sickness have you had?

ROBERT. There is a first for everything and there could be a first here tonight if I could just find someone who was listening to what I was saying.

ANNE. Then tell the lad stories of interest. He's young and full of life just like you were when you were his age. Why don't you tell him stories about you and the Peep O Day Boys.

ROBERT. I never had any dealings with any Peep O Day Boys.

ANNE. God forgive you.

DAVID. Is that not true?

ROBERT. Your grandmother gets a bit muddled with names.

ANNE. Your father was a wild one, David son.

ROBERT. Whether I was or whether I wasn't is unimportant right now.

DAVID. Were you or weren't you?

ROBERT. Let me tell you what is important. And this is a fact if you care to listen. Although I have always been capable, many others through laziness or carelessness find it impossible to tackle their own loom. I can put her up, mount her and rig her out. It is a fine action, both to observe and to do and if you listen to me you will be able to do it for yourself.

ROBERT *stands and begins to pace.*

Never forget there are many complications that can occur as you well know. Accidents do happen. But no matter how careful the workman is, there are incidents that cannot be avoided. Anyone can enter a man's lodgings and with a knife, blade or sharp instrument an enemy could tear your loom and your work would be stopped. If he did it with true malice your family could feel the pain of having to go without while they wait for repairs. During the wait disease could befall them. Disease loves a torn loom and starving children. Now! It could take a man, a clever man, ten days to a fortnight to get himself back up and running. I can do it in a week. Few people possess the necessary skills to carry out this work. I have done it many times, for us and for others, and each time I did it, it was not for kindness or neighbourly goodness, I did it for you and now I want you to learn how to do it for me.

ANNE. What your father tells you, David, is true. Every little bit extra that you can bring into the house will eventually double and treble.

ROBERT (*to* ANNE). You know how important it is. So why do you keep interrupting me and distracting him?

ANNE. It's because you don't tell a good story. You don't make learning interesting for the lad. Don't you see that just making him repeat the words a hundred times over is boring him and turning him away from you.

ROBERT. What do you know about my ways?

ANNE. I'm here listening to you.

ROBERT. I walked him a hundred times until he could stand on his own two feet and walk the length of this house. I held his arms and moved them a thousand times so he could box any man from near or far.

ANNE. I'm not getting at you, Robert. You have created a fine young man in David. What I'm trying to do is stop you from throwing it all away.

ROBERT. Let him decide. Tell me David, where would you rather be? Out there a fool, or in here learning all my secrets and preparing to follow me at the loom.

ANNE. He would prefer a little bit of both or just the one if it could be made a little more interesting. Why not read him some of your poems?

DAVID. No!

ROBERT. Is there something wrong with my poems now, as well?

ANNE. Maybe you would be better to threaten him with a reading every time he got something wrong.

DAVID *laughs.*

ROBERT. That's enough! I've broken my back to afford you everything you desired and now do I have to stand here and be ridiculed?

ANNE *indicates to* DAVID *that it is time to recite his learning.*

DAVID. First every thread has to be tied separately to the beam and then wound on it. Then every thread has to be brought forward and put through the small eyes of the mails on the heddles and then between the teeth of the reed and then tied to the cloth beam.

DAVID *stops and* ROBERT *waits for him to continue.*

ROBERT. Is that it?

DAVID. What else do you want of me?

ROBERT. Tell me one trick.

DAVID. What like?

ANNE (*almost whispering*). Flour and water!

ROBERT. Don't help him.

DAVID. Brush flour and water finely into the threads and fan
them dry.

ANNE. Tallow.

DAVID. Rub them with tallow. Thoroughly.

ROBERT. Why?

DAVID. Why what?

ROBERT. Why do what you just said?

DAVID. Because you told me to.

ROBERT. Yes, I know, but why?

DAVID. Because it's a trick.

ROBERT. Why is it a trick?

DAVID. Because you told me it was.

ROBERT. I told you it was a trick because it is a trick. It's not a
trick just because I told you it was, it's a trick because it
gives a better finish . . .

ANNE. And the dressing dissolves during bleaching.

ROBERT. You have to know all this, David. There's no point in
just rhyming it all off, you have to understand it all. You
could be a master weaver.

DAVID. I don't want to be a master weaver.

ROBERT. What?

DAVID. Nothing.

ROBERT. What did you say there?

DAVID. I just want my tea.

ANNE. Robert let the lad get his tea.

ROBERT. Tell me what you just said.

ANNE. You heard what he said.

ROBERT. I'm not asking you.

DAVID. May I be excused?

ROBERT. Indeed you may not.

ANNE. It's been a hard day, the lad's exhausted, let him go Robert.

ROBERT (*sarcastically*). Are you tired, son? Have you been working too hard, eh, have you? (*Angry.*) You don't know anything about being tired. Where would you be today if I had have crept away to bed whenever I felt tired? Solve this riddle. A man owns a house and a little land. On the land he has a small plot and a cow. He grows flax for the good ladies of the house and gives them the milk from the cow. He works the loom and creates fine linen, which he sells in the markets, where he buys every manner of provision. This man refuses to allow his son to till the land because it will damage the boy's hands and prevent him from producing the finest linen. The man knows his son to be capable, because he has spent all his free time teaching the lad everything that he needs to know. Who is this man?

DAVID. He sounds like a great fellow, if I ever see anybody like that I'll let you know.

ROBERT *moves towards* DAVID *in anger.*

ANNE. Robert?

ROBERT. Don't worry, I won't lift a hand to him. (*Pause.*) I awake every morning and desire to fashion of my son a man of greatness and by the evening I wish I had never fashioned him at all.

DAVID. May I be excused now?

ROBERT. There is no excuse for you. If your mother was alive I would beg her to give me another son.

DAVID. At least you would have that choice. Sons have none with their fathers.

ROBERT. Get out of my sight.

ANNE. Come on and get your tea.

ROBERT. David . . . Rest good and well. After tea we will start all over again.

DAVID *goes into the living room as* ROBERT *paces.*

ANNE. Come on Robert.

DAVID gets himself a mug of tea and sits drinking it at the fire watching the door.

ROBERT. What would Margaret say about this? It's times like this that I really miss her.

ANNE. I know son, but don't be too hard on David, these are difficult times for us all.

ROBERT. I know. I know what it's like to be young. But if Margaret was here he wouldn't be getting on like this.

ANNE. Don't be so hard on yourself either.

ROBERT. Of course he would have a wee brother to set an example for too. What I mean is, I would give my own life in return for theirs. That sounds like one of my poems, I know, but how can I explain it? I wish she was here.

Uncomfortable pause.

She was always better with the children. Ruth as well as David.

ANNE. Here's a riddle for you then. Your father told me that the greatest thing he ever gave you was nothing you could hold, or touch or even see.

ROBERT. That's easy. Everyone knows the gift you can't hold or touch or see. It's life itself.

ANNE. No. God gave you that.

ROBERT. What is it then?

ANNE. Liberty.

As she speaks ANNE leaves the room and enters the living room followed by ROBERT. ANNE gets two mugs of tea and passes one to ROBERT. DAVID walks to the door. ANNE returns to her seat at the fire.

ROBERT. Where are you going?

DAVID. I'm just going to get some air and clear my head.

ROBERT. A man needs powerful lungs and a clear head if he is to work the loom well.

DAVID steps outside and closes the door.

ANNE. You're very like your father. Whenever I yearn for his presence like you with Margaret, I look at you and I see him. He wanted to make you into something so special. He wanted you to be the best.

ROBERT. I know, I have the scars.

ANNE. But he didn't give up, he reached a point in his own mind of enlightenment. That was his word for it, not mine. He set you free. We can only give them so much, Robert. Warnings, beatings, scoldings –

ROBERT. I have never harmed the children.

ANNE. – harsh words, punishments of sorts, whatever. There comes a time when they are out of reach, Robert.

ANNE *begins to embroider cotton muslin.*

ROBERT. I know, I know. I'm not trying to kill him or ruin his life, you know that. I wouldn't let him put his hand into an open fire anymore than I would let him put himself into this Orange Institution.

ANNE. And your father was the same with you.

ROBERT. There was nothing like that then.

ANNE. Hearts of Steel, Steel Boys, Oakboys, call them what you will, they may have changed their names, but it's still the same boys doing the same things.

ROBERT. No, it's not. This is different. This is something that stands against change.

ANNE. Nonsense, it's just another name and the next generation of young men will change it and most of whatever they claim to be fighting for along with it.

ROBERT. I don't know. I just don't know what to do with him.

ANNE. Take him to the Maze at Lisburn.

ROBERT. All the horse meetings have been suspended because of the trouble and the rumours.

ANNE. How long for?

ROBERT. Until further notice.

ANNE. Sure there's been rumours for decades. In fact ever since all the nonsense in America people have talked of little else.

ROBERT. France you mean.

DAVID *comes back into the house.*

ANNE. America. That's where the trouble started.

DAVID. Here comes Ruth. Why don't you ask her where she's been?

ROBERT. I don't need to ask Ruth anything. She's old enough to look after herself and her work in this house has never been found wanting. Now, that is something that you should think about.

DAVID. You should ask her anyway.

ANNE. Why are you hovering at the door, David?

ROBERT. Come away from it, David.

DAVID. I'm getting some air.

ROBERT. I said come away!

> DAVID *comes into the house and walks to the bedroom.*

ANNE. Are you expecting someone?

DAVID. I have to rest.

> DAVID *enters the bedroom.*

ROBERT. A cock fight.

ANNE. What?

ROBERT. I'll take the lad to a cock fight.

ANNE. Your father was always set against it.

ROBERT. I know and I know why. Watching those creatures fight until one of them dies, that's maybe all the lad needs to see to put this talk of war in its proper perspective.

> *Enter* RUTH *and* HARRY. RUTH *moves directly into the living room while* HARRY *hovers at the door.*

HARRY. I'll wait here.

RUTH. Come in.

ROBERT. William?

RUTH. This is Harry, Father.

HARRY. Pleased to make . . . (*your acquaintance*).

ROBERT. Where is William?

RUTH. At home I should think.

HARRY. It's not safe to be out. So, I asked Ruth . . . (*if I could walk her home*).

ROBERT. You will not speak in my house until I speak to you.

RUTH. Father!

ROBERT. I've asked you a question and I'll ask you again. This time I want a proper answer.

RUTH. There was trouble at the tavern and William had to leave.

ROBERT. At the what?

RUTH. The tavern.

HARRY. May I speak with you, sir?

ROBERT. There'll be time for you to speak when Ruth has answered my question.

RUTH. Father, Harry saw me home safely.

ROBERT. I'll speak to you about that, later.

ANNE. Robert, let the gentleman in.

HARRY. If you would permit me, perhaps I could explain.

RUTH. William set a trap for Harry and his friends. The bastards are barricading us into our own homes. They've cut off all the roads and set eyes everywhere to watch us.

ROBERT. I had hoped I would never have lived to hear you use such words.

RUTH. What?

ROBERT. Promise me you will never use that word in my presence again.

RUTH. Father, I am talking to you about the most serious of events and all you have heard is one word.

ROBERT. And I will hear no more until tomorrow.

RUTH. You make me so angry!

ANNE. Ruth! Hold your tongue.

HARRY. Sir! What Ruth says is true. Forgive her anger. Tonight she has witnessed at first hand the ugliness of men.

ROBERT. And you were part of this ugliness.

HARRY. We were in the tavern.

ROBERT. Who are we?

HARRY. Myself and my friends.

ROBERT. Who are your friends?

RUTH. Listen to what he has to say.

ANNE. Ruth!

HARRY. There was a meeting of great importance at the tavern tonight. I was there to guard the premises and to see that no undesirables entered. I failed in this duty when I left my post to speak to William.

ROBERT. What did you speak to him about?

HARRY. We exchanged opinions as to the future of our great country and your daughter.

ROBERT. What is your interest in my daughter, sir?

ANNE. Robert, the gentleman was good enough to see Ruth home safely. Let him get heat at the fire before we send him back out into the cold.

HARRY. You're very kind.

ROBERT. My daughter is to be married to William Hamill.

RUTH. No I'm not.

ANNE. Robert, we had better sit down and try to sort this out.

RUTH. Unless you have another daughter I don't know about.

ROBERT (*to* HARRY). The Hamills are one of the most powerful and dangerous families in these parts. If I was you I'd be a little more careful about who I walked home at night.

HARRY. Sir, I have to say that I find you . . .

RUTH (*interrupts*). I'm not to be married to any such man.

ANNE. Ruth, why don't you introduce the gentleman properly?

ROBERT. I don't need any introductions. I just wish to know what business you have walking my daughter home from the tavern.

HARRY. Sir, I have become acquainted with your daughter ever since she stopped walking with William.

DAVID *opens the door and steps inside.*

ROBERT. Well, it's only a matter of time until they are firmly engaged to be married. So I wouldn't bother entertaining any thoughts of . . .

RUTH. That is not true!

ROBERT. Ruth!

ANNE. Robert, the gentleman –

HARRY. Harry.

ANNE. – Harry, hasn't said anything other than the fact that he wished and did see Ruth home safely.

DAVID. Is that all he did?

RUTH. This is nothing to do with you.

HARRY (*to* ROBERT). That is all I did, sir. Apart from talk.

DAVID. Talk about what?

RUTH. Things you're too young to understand.

ROBERT. Then tell me, I'm surely old enough.

DAVID. Or have you something to hide?

RUTH. I have nothing to hide. And will you just keep out of it?

ANNE. What did you talk about, Harry?

HARRY. We talked about everything really.

ROBERT. Like what?

HARRY. Like the fact that I hope Ruth will agree to share my future and profit me with a family of my own.

ROBERT. That's not possible.

RUTH. Father!

ROBERT. I'm sorry, I must ask you to leave now.

RUTH. Stay where you are, Harry.

ROBERT. Do not disgrace yourself further daughter.

RUTH. It is too late for you to have any say. Harry has asked me for my hand and I have made my decision.

HARRY. You have?

RUTH. I have.

ANNE. Ruth . . .

ROBERT. I asked you to leave.

RUTH. The answer is yes.

ANNE. God help us now.

RUTH. Yes I will marry him and there is little you can do.

> HARRY *is so delighted that he moves towards her.* ROBERT *blocks his way.*

ROBERT. Go any further and you will have to go through me, sir.

> HARRY *stops.*

RUTH. This is not how it should happen, Father, but you have forced it to be this way.

DAVID. You better leave.

HARRY. I'll go when I know the next time I'll meet Ruth.

ROBERT. You will go now or the next time she meets you will be at your funeral.

ANNE. Leave now young man and let this family sort itself out before you seek to enter it.

RUTH. I will meet you tomorrow.

HARRY. I shall leave now. Forgive me madam.

> HARRY *bows to* ANNE *before leaving.* ROBERT *moves to the door.*

ANNE. Before you speak in anger again. Listen and consider what Ruth has to say.

> ROBERT *moves to his seat and sits slowly. He is trying very hard to restrain his anger.*

ROBERT. There is nothing to listen to. Ruth, you will put all this nonsense out of your head and bring no further disgrace to yourself this night or any night in the future.

ANNE. What happened tonight, Ruth?

DAVID. Did your so called friends harm William? Because if they did, they will pay a substantial price.

RUTH. I wish they had, but they stayed their anger.

ROBERT. How honourable.

RUTH. That's the truth. They are the only honourable men to be found in these parts.

ANNE. Tell us the facts and allow us to judge for ourselves young lady.

DAVID. Lady?

RUTH. There was a great meeting at the tavern tonight to hear the news from Dublin. Some of the men who will soon make up our own government attended the meeting.

ROBERT. Ruth, you speak of things you don't understand. These men are clever I grant you that, but their talk is only harmful. They seek to fix things that are not broken.

RUTH. Is not our liberty broken, when men are prevented from assembling together to discuss matters of great importance?

ROBERT. Let me tell you what is of true importance, Ruth. Everything within these walls is of the utmost importance to us. Outside of them nothing can compare.

RUTH. These walls can protect us from the wind but not from tyranny.

DAVID. Father this is the sort of talk that will bring great trouble to our house.

ROBERT. I will not sit here and listen to this for a moment longer. Go to bed, Ruth.

RUTH. Go to bed, Ruth?

ROBERT. I don't know how many times this day you have deceived me or betrayed me, but I tell you now, this is where it ends. Go to bed at once before you give me cause to strike you.

ANNE. You do look very tired, Ruth.

RUTH. I'm tired of this. And I will go to bed and sleep the sleep of the just. Tomorrow I will rise and hope that my fellow countrymen rise with me.

DAVID. Fellow traitors you mean.

RUTH. You don't know what you're talking about, David.

DAVID. I know this much. If they do rise tomorrow then they will fall just as fast.

ROBERT. What are you talking about?

ANNE. What has this to do with you, David?

RUTH *takes a document from her pocket.*

RUTH. This is what it has to do with him.

ROBERT. What is this?

RUTH. If you really want to know about betrayal. Read this!

RUTH *slams the document into* ROBERT*'s hand and leaves.*

ROBERT. What have I done against God, that he has lifted up my children against me?

DAVID. He hasn't lifted me against you.

ANNE. You have done nothing wrong, Robert.

ROBERT. I will have to go and make this right with the Hamills.

ANNE. Why?

ROBERT. This is no way to carry on an engagement.

ANNE. Robert! There is no engagement.

DAVID. Because of her.

ROBERT. We'll work it out.

ANNE. Let me read that.

ROBERT (*to* DAVID). Have you spoken to William?

DAVID. I've listened.

ROBERT. And what has he said?

DAVID. He's hurting.

ROBERT. He's hurting? He'll get over it. So will she.

ANNE. Don't be so sure, Robert.

ROBERT. We have to be sure. We have to keep this Harry fellow
well away from them both.

DAVID. Ruth especially.

ROBERT. They need time to heal. They need time alone –
together.

ANNE. Robert, you can't make things heal.

ROBERT. Maybe not, but you can try.

ANNE. And why should we try so hard if William has lost
interest?

ROBERT. No-one said William had lost interest. Has he David?

DAVID. He might have.

ROBERT. I'm going to call her back out.

ANNE. Leave her, Robert.

ROBERT. This is important.

DAVID. Tell me what you think we should do about this Harry
fellow.

ANNE. You keep away from such matters, David.

ROBERT. If I need to involve you in this David I will, but for
now leave it to me.

ANNE. Why not just leave it to them? Let them sort it out for
themselves.

ROBERT. No, we can't. Bad blood between ourselves and the
Hamills will surely prevent us from obtaining their stamp on
our wares.

ANNE. You have a stamp also, Robert.

ROBERT (*hesitates*). A tit for tat dispute would cause needless hardship.

ROBERT *begins to pace angrily and as he does he begins to read the document to himself. When he reads a little he stops still and looks at* DAVID.

ROBERT. Is this yours? 'We, the loyal inhabitants of the province of Ulster, who have been styled Orangemen in remembrance of our glorious deliverer King William the Third . . .'

ANNE. I can't hear you.

ROBERT. I don't believe this. ' . . . Anxious to co-operate in preserving internal tranquillity and repelling invasion should our foreign enemies be desperate enough to attempt it, we take this opportunity of declaring our readiness to undertake any duty in obedience to the commands of his Excellency the Lord Lieutenant.'

ANNE. What?

ROBERT. David!

DAVID. That's our declaration.

ANNE. What declaration?

ROBERT. Have you signed one of these?

DAVID. You don't have to sign it.

ANNE. What do you have to do with it?

DAVID. You take an oath.

ANNE. Have you taken an oath?

ROBERT. They're going to take you away, David. This is what this means. This Orange Institution, I warned you about it, but you wouldn't listen.

DAVID. They're not taking me away anywhere. The whole point of it is that we stay here.

ROBERT. David! This means trouble. More than that, if there is trouble, you will be the first to be sent in. Do you think that this is some sort of honour, to go in first, to be the bravest? It's simply the quickest way to get yourself killed.

ANNE. Where did you hear of this?

DAVID. William told me about it.

ANNE. There's your Hamills for you, Robert.

ROBERT. What do you think this is?

DAVID. The Grand Master, Mr Hamill, says that the United
Irishmen are coming to destroy our country and kill us all.

ANNE. I don't know what they've been filling your head with,
David, but I don't believe I like it.

DAVID. Father, we have to defend Ireland.

ROBERT. I beg your pardon.

DAVID. We're all in it together.

ROBERT. Let me explain something to you, David. I own this
house and everything in it. When I die I will pass it on to
you. So, be very sure, that this house and everything to do
with it is the only part of Ireland that we need to protect.

DAVID. That's nonsense.

ROBERT. I don't think it is, I believe it is fact and if you don't
like it . . .

DAVID. What if everybody took that attitude and left us
unprotected here. The Unitedmen would come and burn our
house down with us in it.

ROBERT (*holding the declaration high*). This is a serious
business, David.

DAVID. There is nothing more serious than a man serving his
King.

ROBERT. Is that what you think this is?

DAVID. I know it is.

ROBERT. I've already lost one son to God. Tell me that I did not
build this house and our business so as you could walk away
and die for a stranger.

DAVID. When did the King become a stranger?

ROBERT. The King will not be fighting in this battle, son.

DAVID. We're fighting *for* the King, Father. The scum that your
own daughter never stops talking about are fighting *against*
our King. Maybe you should be lecturing her.

ROBERT. If she ever decides to risk her life for no good reason
then I will lecture her.

DAVID. Do you hear what you're saying, Father? The King is no good reason.

ANNE. Why don't we sit down and talk properly?

DAVID. I've no time, I'm going to go out.

ROBERT. You're going nowhere.

ANNE. Come on the both of you and sit down.

DAVID. I volunteered for the night watch so as it wouldn't interfere with work. So did William.

ANNE. That's who you've been watching for.

DAVID. He was supposed to meet me here but maybe he decided not to bother because of this business in the tavern.

ROBERT. You're not old enough to volunteer for anything.

DAVID. I am old enough.

ROBERT. Would you listen to him?

ANNE. I hear every word he says, do you?

ROBERT. What?

DAVID. And have you heard every word he has said?

ANNE. I have.

ROBERT. You must be the only one. I'm beginning to think I've raised two deaf children.

DAVID. You have troubles of your own.

ROBERT. Apparently more than I had imagined.

DAVID. I am going into town to help you with some of those troubles.

ROBERT. I'll sort my own troubles out.

DAVID. Answer me this. When's the Weaver's great march across town?

ROBERT. Wednesday fortnight after market day, why what has that to do with it?

DAVID. It has everything to do with it. This great march that you're always going on about won't be happening on that day or any other day for that matter.

ROBERT. Of course it will, it's traditional. We'll walk to town with gentlemen at the head and drummers at the back. Our colours will be visible for miles. What will you say when you see that?

DAVID. Father! Since martial law was imposed, all gatherings of more than four people have been declared unlawful. That would include a march. So you may keep your flags and banners and your best clothes for another year, that's if we ever return to normality, because let me tell you this, Father. If you and many like you don't wake up soon, you will never march through the town again. Not for the Duke of Cumberland, not in memory of any great victory over the rebel armies, not ever. That's the work of this United Irish Society. That's what they are about.

ROBERT. But I've heard that many of them are weavers.

ANNE. Many of them are Protestant, you can't deny that.

ROBERT. Johnston himself, a man I know you respect greatly told me that their leaders are all Protestant.

DAVID. Sure you would call yourself a Protestant.

ROBERT. What's that supposed to mean?

DAVID. You call yourself a Protestant and yet you mock the King and the willingness of men like me to fight on his behalf.

ROBERT. No, no. I was saying that to keep you here because of your youth.

DAVID. Well, the point is there are Protestants and then there are real Protestants.

ANNE. Is that what you are?

ROBERT. Styled Orange after your King William?

DAVID. That's correct.

ROBERT. David, you don't understand.

DAVID. I understand this. Any Protestant, having knowledge of the horrors that have been carried out in Wexford where Protestant men, women and children were brutally and savagely destroyed, having possession of such knowledge and not affording himself to react valiantly, in my eyes he is worse than any Catholic.

ROBERT. What do you know about Wexford?

DAVID. I know that a Catholic Priest led the very scum of the earth against the innocent Protestant people. They destroyed them all. They rent their limbs asunder, poked out their eyes and carried out all manner of executions unimaginable in our civilised minds.

ANNE. That's hearsay and story telling.

DAVID. You hear it the way you want to hear it and I'll hear it the way I know to be true.

WILLIAM *slams hard on the door before entering.*

WILLIAM. David?

ROBERT. Come in, son.

WILLIAM *acknowledges* ANNE *with a bow.*

WILLIAM. Sir, your son and I are requested to present ourselves immediately for inspection.

ROBERT. William come in and sit down.

DAVID. I better get ready.

WILLIAM. Be quick about it. My father's expecting trouble in town.

DAVID *puts on a pair of boots.*

ANNE. What's going on, William?

WILLIAM. It's started.

ROBERT. What has?

WILLIAM. The rebellion.

ANNE. Lord help us.

ROBERT. He said you were going on the night watch.

WILLIAM. News has this evening reached my father that the French are due to land and it's his opinion that Belfast will follow Antrim and Down with the Unitedmen attacking every Protestant house from one end of Ireland to the other.

DAVID. What did I tell you, Father?

ANNE. But many of the Unitedmen are Protestant.

WILLIAM. Presbyterian traitors are no more Protestant than the Pope himself.

ROBERT. Don't be in such a hurry. The French have been landing for years, but they never do.

WILLIAM. Join us Mister Moore and we shall fight the true fight together.

DAVID. Yes, Father, it is never too late to join us. What a sight it would be, father and son standing side by side fighting the enemies of their King and God.

ANNE. I have read a great deal of these men and they beg to be thought of as representing all religions.

WILLIAM. That's not possible.

DAVID. What do you say, Father?

ROBERT. Everything that I have read about these Unitedmen I found to contain clumsy politics.

WILLIAM. In Leinster and Wexford our brothers in the Orange have died at the hands of the Papists. Tell *them* that it is not a religious uprising.

ANNE. William, sit with us, we have other things to discuss.

WILLIAM. We have to go. Are you coming?

DAVID *senses that* ROBERT *is staying.*

DAVID. Maybe it would be better for us all if you stayed here and watched this place. We will need guards everywhere. Is someone guarding your house, William?

WILLIAM. My grandfather is too old and frail, he has to stay behind.

DAVID. Then my father will be our eyes and ears in these parts. Father, I would ask only this of you, that you would on occasion look in on William's grandfather.

ANNE. Robert, make them stay.

ROBERT. William, have you spoken to your father about Ruth?

WILLIAM. That matter is closed for now, sir.

ANNE. Speak to us.

ROBERT. You know what we desire for you.

WILLIAM. My feelings have changed in that matter. I no longer wish to chase after Ruth and must insist that we leave now before I find myself in battle with this house.

ANNE. What do you mean?

ROBERT. Why would you do that?

WILLIAM. There are things I love in this house. I respect yourself and your mother and all the great work that has been produced here. I owe the same debt my father for your stamp and consider David's friendship to be of great value, but I must admit that I have brought great shame on my family in my pursuit of your daughter. She has embarrassed and humiliated me and my name far and wide.

DAVID. Talk no more about it. Let's go!

ROBERT. Tell me what your father has said on the matter.

WILLIAM. He will hear no more about it and has instructed me to stay from speaking or acting on it, leaving these things to him.

DAVID. Come on, William. We can talk about all this later.

ANNE. You might look at things different after a little time.

WILLIAM. I fear not.

DAVID. Come on!

WILLIAM. I must go, Sir. Thinking of her only causes me great sorrow.

WILLIAM turns and rushes away. DAVID hugs his father.

DAVID. Know this, Father. We can sort all manner of difference between us when I return.

ROBERT. Son, tell William I will call on his grandfather as often as possible.

ANNE. Can we say anything that would keep you near?

DAVID. I have to go. You guard here, I will guard you from afar.

WILLIAM. David!

They leave.

ROBERT. I have prayed a thousand times for God to keep this day from me.

ANNE. Now we have to deal with it.

ROBERT. The young are as brave as they are foolish.

ANNE. Pray only now for his safety.

ROBERT. What could I have said or done to make him stay?

ANNE. Nothing!

ROBERT. I have often dreamed that we struggled at the door. Him to go and fight, I to make him stay and work.

ANNE. What happened?

ROBERT. Dreams are only dreams. The truth is I could not bring myself to dishonour him.

ANNE. He will return. You told me yourself the Unitedmen had no support near here. Now, come on, sit down.

ROBERT. That is true. Well, that is what I thought was true until tonight.

Enter RUTH, *fully dressed.*

RUTH. Father, did I hear our David leave?

ROBERT. Yes, he left with William.

RUTH. Didn't you read the declaration that I gave you?

ROBERT. I read it.

RUTH. And you still let him go.

ANNE. There was nothing we could do to stop him.

ROBERT. Go back to bed, Ruth.

RUTH. Did they say where they were going?

ROBERT. That's of no concern to you.

ANNE. They didn't.

RUTH *paces.*

RUTH. I have to go out!

ROBERT. What?

ANNE. Where have you to go?

ROBERT. Would you leave this house during the night to bring great shame on us all?

RUTH. The shame of this house left just minutes ago.

ANNE. Don't speak like that of your brother.

RUTH. You know what they are going to do, don't you? They have gone to steal, destroy, rape and murder. For the fame of the Orange Institution goes before them.

ANNE. And are you going to warn their enemies?

RUTH. Harry and his friends will be unprepared and undefended.

ROBERT. You will have no further business with this Harry fellow.

RUTH. Father! I love him. I love him with a true and pure love. That is why I must go and warn him.

ROBERT. Have you no self respect or dignity left?

RUTH. Have you? Letting your son involve himself with the Hamills and you yourself freely giving your stamp to them. What dignity is that?

ROBERT. Don't you speak to me like that young woman.

RUTH. I should have left with Harry.

ANNE. Where would you go?

RUTH. Anywhere is better than here.

ANNE. But if this revolution is so great then won't it come here too?

ROBERT. This revolution is going to bring only death wherever people are foolish enough to entertain such dreams and folly.

RUTH. What are we if we cannot dream?

ANNE. You should hold your tongue and pay respect to your elders.

RUTH. I wish I could. My entire body wishes it were easy, but how can I pay my respects when I am held here in service to my own family against my will?

ROBERT. What are you talking about?

RUTH. I have stayed here and worked to help you. Harry advised me to do so for he is a man of goodwill.

ROBERT. I don't want to hear any more about this Harry fellow. He's probably got foolish young women in every town that has a tavern.

RUTH. You don't know him and you don't know his like.

ROBERT. I think I know him too well. Men like that, full of stories and bravado are a penny a hundred.

RUTH. If that was true the revolution would have happened years ago.

ROBERT. And why has it not? Solve that riddle. Why has this glorious day been so long in the coming? I'll solve it for you. The men you speak so highly of have no followers.

RUTH. No followers? You know so little for such a clever man.

ROBERT. Only outcasts and foolish gentlemen with too much time on their hands would even consider such notions as revolution.

ANNE. And I can name no women who would support such men.

RUTH. I will tell you secret information that must never leave this house, if you will promise to hold it.

ROBERT. What information?

RUTH. You must promise for this information can lead to great
sorrow in the wrong hands.

ANNE. Promise Robert.

ROBERT. All right, I promise.

RUTH. The news from Dublin is that within days Wolfe Tone
will land with a French force of twenty thousand men. Henry
Joy McCracken will lead an army of ten thousand men.
Munro has seven thousand under his command and each time
they take a town their ranks will swell until no-one will have
to live under the reign of the King or any figure put in his
place. Soon we will see the commencement of the first year
of liberty.

ANNE. God save us.

ROBERT. Ruth, have you any idea how many times we have
heard stories like that?

ANNE. But it's all history now, isn't it?

RUTH. History is about to change more drastically than you
have ever imagined.

ROBERT. I seem to remember this Tone fellow was on ship with
a great army a couple of years ago. Yet here we are still the
same people, living the same lives in the same country.

RUTH. England's interest here only survived because of so
many coincidences. This time luck will not be on its side.

ANNE. Don't talk about England like that.

RUTH. It hurts my heart to speak of it at all.

ROBERT. We have a lot to thank our English friends for.

RUTH. Don't! I would rather put myself to death than thank the
English.

ANNE. Is this the nonsense this Harry fellow has been filling
your head full of?

RUTH. It is called learning.

ANNE. Is that what you learned instead of respect and manners?

RUTH. Outside these doors a trap is being prepared. You, like
many others are going to believe the lies about the rebellion
starting and about countless deaths and murders of Protestants

that simply did not happen. Believe this. The Orange are going to attack innocent men and slay them in their beds tonight.

ROBERT. But you've just told us that these innocent men are plotting insurrection.

RUTH. The rebellion will take the shape of an honourable battle. If it meets any resistance – which it shouldn't – our men will fight fairly and properly as gentlemen.

ANNE. Ruth, think about what you're saying.

RUTH. I know exactly what I'm saying. I have to go and warn Harry.

ROBERT. That's out of the question.

RUTH. Well, I can't stay here and wait for the knowledge of his death to come through that door probably from the mouth of my own brother.

ROBERT *blocks her path.*

ROBERT. There is nothing we can do about what happens outside of this house. Now, I have already failed to prevent one member of this family leaving the sanctuary of my home . . .

RUTH. I have to go.

ROBERT. You have to go to bed.

RUTH. Don't be ridiculous.

RUTH *walks towards the door.*

ROBERT. Where do you think you're going? Ruth you will come back here this minute young woman. Ruth!

ANNE. Robert she's really going to go.

ROBERT. Ruth, do not take another step or so help me . . .

RUTH *stops at the door.*

RUTH. What?

ANNE. Ruth, don't go.

ROBERT. If you step outside that door you are no daughter of mine. I mean it.

ANNE. Ruth, love . . .

ROBERT. And another thing. Don't think you can ever step back in again.

RUTH. You have ears yet you do not hear. You've got eyes that do not see. Don't you understand that I have no choice? If I stay here and something happens to Harry, this family would be torn apart forever. This way there is hope.

ROBERT. Ruth . . .

RUTH. Forgive me.

RUTH *steps outside and walks away leaving the door open.*
ROBERT *rushes to the door then stands and watches her go.*

ROBERT. What am I going to do?

ANNE. Go after her.

ROBERT. I can't.

ROBERT *paces the room.* ANNE *follows him with her eyes.*

Lights dim and go to black.

ACT TWO

Dawn.

ANNE *is sleeping by the fire when* RUTH *and* HARRY *enter.* HARRY *checks the work room as* RUTH *goes to her bedroom.*

RUTH *returns with two dresses and places them on a sheet. As* HARRY *returns to the living room* RUTH *points towards* ANNE *to alert him to her presence then* RUTH *places a pair of shoes beside the dresses.* RUTH *then goes to the fire place and lifts a small locket while* HARRY *wraps her belongings in the sheet and ties it firmly around them. He meets* RUTH *half way and they walk towards the door.*

ANNE. Not even a good bye?

    RUTH *and* HARRY *stop at the door.* ANNE *sits up.*

RUTH. We have to leave.

HARRY. We could stay a while if you're frightened.

ANNE. What have I to be frightened of?

RUTH. Terrible things have happened this night. That is why we can't stay.

ANNE. I didn't ask you to stay.

RUTH. Come on Harry.

HARRY. Is there anything you wish of us before we leave, Madam?

ANNE. An explanation would be nice.

RUTH. There's no time.

    RUTH *stands at the door.* HARRY *steps towards* ANNE.

HARRY. We have seen horrible things.

RUTH. Harry?

ANNE. Was it the Orangemen?

RUTH. Who else?

ANNE. Did you see David?

HARRY. No.

RUTH. All we've seen is murder and slaughter.

HARRY. Where is Ruth's father?

ANNE. He has gone to check on the Hamills again. The last time he checked of course being Ruth's father he discovered other people who had to be checked as well and so he has spent the entire night to-ing and fro-ing between all the old people who are unable or too sensible to be involved in this madness.

HARRY. Would you like us to wait until he returns?

RUTH. We can't.

ANNE. Have you eaten?

HARRY. Not today.

ANNE. You can't travel on empty stomachs. Let me get you something.

RUTH. No.

HARRY. It's all right, Ruth. We could eat and we could watch over your Grandmother at the same time.

RUTH. We can't be here when Father returns.

ANNE. At least have some oat cakes. I made plenty, to get me through this night.

HARRY. You're very kind.

ANNE. Will you have some Ruth and I'll brew the tea again?

RUTH. Am I talking to myself? Or to this wall perhaps.

HARRY. You should eat something. We may not get another chance until we get to Belfast.

ANNE. Belfast?

RUTH. You must never tell a soul where we're going.

ANNE. Ruth, love, do you think I helped your father raise you up so as I could cause you harm?

RUTH. Swear on the Bible.

HARRY. There's no need for that.

HARRY *begins to eat the oat cakes.*

RUTH. You can't tell Father or especially not David.

ANNE. I will tell no-one.

RUTH. Swear it.

HARRY. Ruth eat!

ANNE. What have you packed?

HARRY. We can only bring what we can carry.

RUTH. I can carry these. Let's go Harry.

> RUTH *picks up as many oat cakes as she can.*

ANNE. Ruth you have made your decision and I respect that. You are not a prisoner here, you never have been. Come and talk with me for a few minutes, I only want to give you something to take with you. Something you should have with you. I promise I will not try to convince you to stay. And I'll not try to change your mind in any other way. But it would pain me so if we parted on bad terms.

> ANNE *gets up, fully dressed and walks to the bedroom.*

RUTH. But if Father returns.

ANNE. If your father returns he will have to do the same.

HARRY. Talk to her, Ruth.

> ANNE *returns with a bundle from the bedroom. She places it on the table and begins to unwrap it. It is a long white dress.*

RUTH. What is that?

ANNE. It was your Mother's.

HARRY. It's beautiful.

ANNE. She would want you to have it.

RUTH. I can't.

ANNE. And the sheet was the first that your father managed to get stamped. I'll just set these here, if you want them you can take them with you, but if you don't, then you can leave them here.

RUTH. Where are you going now?

> ANNE *searches for and finds a small, old bible.*

ANNE. Take this!

> RUTH *sits down, stunned.*

HARRY. What's the matter, Ruth?

ANNE. This is the first book that . . .

RUTH. I know what it is.

ANNE. (*to* HARRY) She used it to help David with his reading. And this . . .

ANNE *produces an old piece of cloth.*

RUTH. That's enough!

ANNE. She was making . . . What were you making again?

Silence.

ANNE. Ruth?

RUTH *turns away to hide her pain.*

HARRY. What is that?

ANNE. She was making something for her new brother when Margaret – that's Ruth's mother – she went in to labour and that was the last time Ruth saw her alive.

RUTH. A handkerchief. It was going to be a handkerchief.

ANNE *takes a ring from her finger.*

ANNE. And this will remind you of me.

RUTH (*jumps to her feet*). I don't want it. I don't want any of it.

ANNE *reaches it towards* RUTH. RUTH *walks to the door and opens it.*

ANNE. It might bring you a little bit of luck.

RUTH *stops at the door.*

RUTH. Let's go Harry. Please!

ANNE. It certainly brought me a lot of luck since your grandfather gave me it. Until now of course. Perhaps it doesn't work for me any more. That could be another reason for you to have it.

HARRY *begins to gather up everything – including the ring. As he takes the ring from* ANNE. ANNE *grasps his hand.*

ANNE. Can I trust you to look after my granddaughter?

HARRY. I will always put her needs before my own.

ANNE *releases his hand.*

RUTH. My father's coming, Harry. Let's go.

ANNE. Why don't you stay and say good-bye to him properly?

RUTH. If we go now we can rush away before he gets close.

HARRY. Maybe we should talk to him.

RUTH. About what?

ANNE. Give him a chance Ruth. You'll probably find him acting different when he gets here and sees that you're set to leave. He's been doing a lot of thinking about it and you know your father when he starts thinking. He's written a poem about you and David. I don't think it's finished yet but don't let this be the way it finishes.

ROBERT is running towards the door. RUTH steps away from it and comes back into the living room.

RUTH. Here he comes.

Enter ROBERT.

ROBERT. I thought I saw you at the door, Ruth.

ROBERT comes in and looks around weighing up the situation.

ROBERT. What's all this?

RUTH. We're leaving.

ROBERT. No, no.

ANNE. You can't stop her, Robert. The only thing we can do is talk.

RUTH. We just have to go.

ROBERT. You can't leave this house. There's trouble all over.

RUTH. That's why we have to leave.

HARRY. They're looking for us.

ROBERT. They're looking for you, you mean.

RUTH. They're looking for us both.

ROBERT. Listen to me, Ruth. There is nowhere to go.

RUTH. I know a place.

HARRY. Maybe it is too dangerous.

ROBERT. It is most definitely too dangerous.

RUTH. Well, it's just going to get worse, Father.

ANNE. How?

RUTH. The English are expected to arrive here in a few days.

ROBERT. Well that might bring some law and order back to this place.

RUTH. You have no idea what you're talking about.

HARRY. Your father has a point Ruth. You're always better dealing with real soldiers.

ROBERT. Listen to me Ruth. Hamill seems to be the head of the Orangemen in these parts. Now, he's known you since you were a baby. If you just stay here, you'll be safe.

ANNE. Your father can talk to him.

RUTH. And what about Harry?

ROBERT. What about you Harry?

HARRY. Sir, if you can assure me that Ruth would be safe here –

RUTH. Harry, no!

HARRY. – then I will leave alone.

ROBERT. Of course she'll be safe.

RUTH. It doesn't matter. I'm not staying here.

HARRY. Listen, Ruth.

ANNE. Listen to him Ruth.

HARRY. I could travel faster on my own. I could go to Belfast and wait.

RUTH. No!

HARRY. As your father says. If the English get here . . .

RUTH. We'll have to fight them too.

ROBERT. Ruth, would you just listen to what you're being told?

ANNE. Let Harry go and hide. When this is over he could come back and we could start over again. Isn't that true, Robert?

ROBERT. If this man leaves here now. When he returns I assure you he will receive a different reception from me.

HARRY. What say you, Ruth?

RUTH. Are you people mad? Have you any idea what you're saying? There's a war out there. Our friends are being slaughtered in their beds by their neighbours.

ROBERT. That's not a war. A war is when enemies meet on the battlefield. What we have here is a massacre, the Orange have all the power in this area and for miles around it. They will win and anyone who supports the rebellion will die.

RUTH. And do you think I could live in a country like that?

ROBERT (*to* HARRY). Do you see what you've done?

HARRY. What?

ROBERT. Do you see what you've filled her head full of?

HARRY. Sir?

ANNE. It seems to me that Harry is trying to help us.

ROBERT. Well, it seems to me that it's not working. And it also seems to me that I'm going to lose my daughter. So, maybe I should take you outside and show her what sort of a man she's getting involved with.

RUTH. Do you see! I knew this would happen if we stayed. Let's go, Harry.

HARRY. I have no fight with you, sir.

ROBERT. Do you not?

HARRY. No.

> ROBERT *stands.*

ROBERT. Stand up.

ANNE. Robert sit down.

ROBERT. Come on.

> ROBERT *slaps* HARRY *across the face. Then grabs at him.* HARRY *tries to keep calm and still.* ROBERT *pushes him back in his seat and turns away in anger.*

ANNE. Robert for goodness sake.

ROBERT. He's caused all this. And I say it's time for him and his like to start paying for all the damage they've done.

RUTH. What damage?

ROBERT. Stealing daughters from their fathers. And probably sons from their mothers.

RUTH. Is that what you think?

ROBERT. That's what I know. (*To* HARRY.) You sir are the worst scum on God's green earth.

> ROBERT *slaps* HARRY *again.*

ROBERT. Get up and fight! Come on!

HARRY. As I have said . . .

> ROBERT *slaps* HARRY *again.*

ROBERT. Are you afraid?

RUTH *moves towards* ROBERT.

HARRY. Stay away Ruth.

ANNE. Robert what are you doing? This isn't going to do any good.

ROBERT. Are you a coward as well as a liar? Are you?

As ROBERT *goes to hit* HARRY *again* HARRY *reacts in anger and forces himself up and backwards from his chair producing his pistol as he does so.*

HARRY. Stay where you are.

RUTH. Harry, let's just get out of here.

ROBERT. That's no more than I expect from your kind. Using weapons against an unarmed opponent. Is that the kind of fight you like? Is that the kind of battle you were hoping for?

RUTH. Come on, Harry!

RUTH *moves to the door.*

HARRY. Outside these walls. Out there! My dreams are dying. My dreams for the future of this great country are being butchered – slaughtered – destroyed. And to answer your question – the kind of war I wanted was a war for the hearts and minds of men and women. But if that war couldn't be fought the way we wanted then we would meet our enemies on the battlefield and fight an honourable fight.

ROBERT. What do you know about honour?

HARRY. What do you think I'm doing? What is it that you think I'm filling Ruth's head full of?

RUTH. You're not filling my head full of anything.

HARRY. I'll tell you what I told her. My desires for this country were simply this. I wanted every man to be equal. No matter where he comes from. No matter what he looks like and no matter how he worships God or which God he worships for that matter. Or maybe a man doesn't want to worship God at all.

ROBERT. That's heresy!

HARRY. To me it's liberty. To me it's about being free. Free from religion, free from bondage. Free from slavery.

ROBERT. There is no slavery.

HARRY. Isn't that what we are, Mister Moore? Slaves? Slaves to the King. Slaves to the English. Shouldn't an Irish man be free to decide the fate of Ireland?

ANNE. You said were!

HARRY. What?

ANNE. You said they were your desires.

RUTH. He meant are.

Silence.

HARRY. I'm ashamed to say but I meant were.

RUTH. It's not over yet, Harry.

HARRY. It is for me.

RUTH. What do you mean?

HARRY. Your father's right. I'm a fraud.

RUTH. You are not. You're just trying to trick me because you're worried about my safety.

HARRY. All the things I said, Ruth. Everything that I believed. It's all faded away.

RUTH. I'm not listening.

ANNE. Listen to him, Ruth.

HARRY. When I met you and we started walking together it put things into a different light. It was as though you filled up that part of my heart that I had given to Ireland. I found myself unable to think of Ireland without picturing you. I found myself unable to think of anything without thinking of you. And now. After this night when I have witnessed for myself the ugliness of the world, I know that I need you. I need you to be safe. If anything ever happened to you because of me I would damn my own soul to hell. (*To* ROBERT.) And that sir is my crime.

HARRY *turns the pistol in his hand and offers it to* ROBERT. ROBERT *doesn't move.*

RUTH. What are you doing?

HARRY *sets the pistol in front of* ROBERT.

Pause.

ROBERT *picks the pistol up and begins to break it up in anger before throwing it at the wall.*

ANNE. What are you going to do, Robert?

ROBERT. I have to go and check on other people.

> ROBERT *walks to the door.*

> I would appreciate it if you would stay and watch my mother while I'm gone. If you're here when I come back, we'll talk but if you're not . . .

> ROBERT *walks out of the house leaving the door open behind him.* ANNE *goes to the door and bolts it shut.* ANNE *begins to make more tea as* HARRY *and* RUTH *wait.*

HARRY. Maybe you should just stay here, Ruth.

RUTH. No Harry, I have to leave this place forever.

ANNE. Where would you go?

RUTH. France, perhaps.

ANNE. You wouldn't survive in France. I've heard that since the revolution people have been starving to death.

RUTH. You've heard a lot of nonsense then.

HARRY. I've been to France myself and although I found it to be wonderful I agree that it's not appropriate for Ruth.

RUTH. This is just another example of why we have to leave. I'm so tired of having to live with the English interpretation of everything.

ANNE. What do you mean?

RUTH. You just saying that you've heard that people are starving to death in France.

ANNE. That is what I've heard.

RUTH. Where did you hear it, from who?

ANNE. I can't remember.

RUTH. News of the world comes to Ireland from England. And that means we get it all from the Englishman's point of view. If the English want us to believe that people are dying in France as a result of the revolution then that's what we are going to be told.

HARRY. The spread of information does work that way. Mostly it would be generated in London.

ANNE. I don't need a lecture on where news comes from. I hear things from my friends and they've heard it from their friends.

RUTH. But if you keep going, eventually you will find that someone somewhere heard it from an Englishman.

HARRY. I think the point that Ruth is trying to make is that the English influence filters into every part of our life and that will inform our opinions and ultimately our judgement about certain things.

RUTH. About everything. Everything is tarnished with Englishness. Irishness is disappearing.

ANNE. Well my point is not influenced by the English. My point is that I just don't want you to go to France.

HARRY. Neither do I.

RUTH. We can talk about it later, Harry.

ANNE. So, I'll never actually know where you are, or if you're alive or dead, I'll just have to guess or maybe ask an Englishman about you, but I suppose he would only tell me what he thought from his point of view.

HARRY. Wherever we go, we will write and let you know where we are and that we're all right.

ANNE. If you are all right.

RUTH. We won't be all right if we stay here.

ANNE. You would.

RUTH. No. I think if we're going to live anywhere it would be somewhere far away from England. Maybe America.

HARRY. I don't know. The journey is long and hazardous.

ANNE. France would be better than America.

RUTH. Well make up your mind. Two minutes ago we would starve to death if we went to France.

SAMUEL *bangs on the door loudly.*

RUTH. Oh my God!

ANNE. That might be your father back.

RUTH. It's too soon.

SAMUEL. Open the door!

RUTH. Harry, you'll have to hide.

HARRY. Where?

More banging and mumbling at the door.

ANNE. Go into the bedroom.

RUTH. No! Walk by me into the work room and as I open that door, I'll close the other door and then I'll guide them in here.

ANNE. Go quickly, Ruth.

HARRY passes RUTH and enters the work room. As SAMUEL shouts again RUTH opens the door. WILLIAM enters the house with SAMUEL. They are carrying DAVID.

SAMUEL. Where is Robert?

ANNE. He's at your house. What's happened to David?

WILLIAM. He's been stabbed in the back.

ANNE. Place him here at the fire.

DAVID moans as they place him near the fire.

SAMUEL. We have clothed the wound twice already, but I'm afraid the bleeding won't cease.

ANNE attempts to inspect the wound. DAVID moans in agony.

WILLIAM. We'll have to stand him up.

SAMUEL. Lie him down.

WILLIAM. But this is how I found him. The only way to stop the pain was for him to be upright.

ANNE. Put him on the bench.

DAVID. Father, Father.

ANNE. You're all right, David son. Don't try to speak.

They struggle to place him in a pain free position.

SAMUEL. I still think we should put him flat on the ground.

WILLIAM. No, he's in too much pain when he lies down.

ANNE sits beside him keeping him upright on the chair.

ANNE. Without help the boy will die.

RUTH. Couldn't you do something?

DAVID. Is that you, Mother?

SAMUEL. The nearest aid would be twenty miles.

WILLIAM. We couldn't risk another mile, we are lucky to have got this far.

SAMUEL. Is there anything you can do, Anne?

ANNE. I have attended many births . . . and deaths, but I know nothing of wounds.

SAMUEL. Then all that remains is prayer.

WILLIAM. What good will that do?

SAMUEL. We can pray for God's will to be done.

WILLIAM. But he doesn't deserve this. You saw how courageously he fought today, Father.

SAMUEL. God has need of courage.

ANNE. Was courage the cause of this?

SAMUEL. I'm afraid so.

WILLIAM. The cause of this was the United scum.

DAVID. Who is that I hear?

ANNE. Be quiet.

WILLIAM. It's me, David.

ANNE. William, there is water at the door. Fetch it, please.

> WILLIAM *rushes out the door.* DAVID *moans.* SAMUEL *produces some wine.*

SAMUEL. Give him this to still the pain.

ANNE. What is it?

SAMUEL. It's a little wine.

> ANNE *assists* DAVID *to drink. He splutters.* WILLIAM *returns with a bucket of water.*

ANNE. Is it cold?

WILLIAM. Yes!

> WILLIAM *places the bucket of water at* ANNE's *side.* ANNE *begins to tear strips of cloth.*

ANNE (*to* DAVID). This will cool the fever, David.

> SAMUEL *moves to the door.* ANNE *leaves a piece of cloth on* DAVID's *forehead and attempts to help him drink more wine.*

SAMUEL. How long has Robert been gone?

ANNE. He has been back and forth constantly.

SAMUEL. When was the last time?

RUTH. Not long ago.

DAVID. Who's that?

ANNE. David, it's Ruth. (*To* RUTH.) Come on over to your brother.

RUTH *kneels beside* DAVID.

RUTH. Is he going to be all right?

ANNE *shakes her head.*

SAMUEL. He has a better chance of surviving with his family around him.

DAVID. Is that Ruth?

RUTH. Yes, David it's me.

DAVID. Ruth!

SAMUEL. I'm going to leave now.

WILLIAM. Where are you going to go?

SAMUEL. I have to go back to the men.

RUTH. Then go!

ANNE *tugs at* RUTH.

DAVID. Don't be angry with us, Ruth.

WILLIAM (*to* SAMUEL). What'll *I* do?

RUTH. Why don't you go too?

SAMUEL. It's up to you, son. If you want to come with me, we'll have to go now. But if you want to stay with David . . . That's a matter for you to decide.

WILLIAM *looks away from his father and watches the two women trying to comfort* DAVID. DAVID *cries out in agony.*

DAVID. Father! Father!

RUTH *dabs the cloth on his head as* ANNE *holds him down.*

WILLIAM. I don't know.

HARRY *enters the living room when* DAVID *screams in agony again.* SAMUEL *immediately takes his pistol in hand and points it at* HARRY.

HARRY. Is he all right? Is he badly hurt?

HARRY *stops short of crossing* SAMUEL.

RUTH. Harry, what are you doing?

WILLIAM. I don't believe this.

SAMUEL. What?

WILLIAM. This! This is the scum of the earth.

SAMUEL. What are you talking about?

RUTH. Be quiet, William.

HARRY. May I see the patient, please?

ANNE. Are you a physician?

HARRY. No, but I know where one is to be found.

WILLIAM. This is a trick.

HARRY. This is no trick. Let me look at him.

ANNE. Ruth, is that true?

> RUTH *watches* HARRY *cross and kneel at the other side of* ANNE. *She looks at him in both pain and disbelief.*

WILLIAM. This is the man I told you about. The man from the Tavern.

SAMUEL. Are you a liar as well as a thief of hearts, sir?

HARRY. As I have said, if I have your permission I will go and get my friend the physician.

SAMUEL. Where is this friend?

RUTH. They're not far. Let him go.

WILLIAM. He's going nowhere.

SAMUEL. Sir, I will permit you to leave if you will permit my son to accompany you on your journey.

RUTH. No!

SAMUEL. It is extremely dangerous outside. My men are hunting down every last Unitedman and putting them to death. William here is widely known and will be able to ensure your safe return.

WILLIAM. I'm staying here.

RUTH. I could go with him.

> WILLIAM *laughs out loud.*

SAMUEL. William, you will accompany this gentleman as I have already instructed. Do you hear me?

WILLIAM (*hesitates*). I do.

DAVID *begins to come around slowly.*

DAVID. Is this a dream?

ANNE. Do you see me?

DAVID. Yes, I do.

ANNE. Then it's not a dream.

DAVID. How did I get home?

SAMUEL. Try not to speak too much, son. You will only aggravate your condition.

DAVID. Yes, sir.

ANNE. Do you want another drink? A nod will be sufficient.

DAVID. No.

RUTH. You're going to be all right, David.

ROBERT *hurries into the house.*

ROBERT. What's happened?

WILLIAM. David's been wounded.

ROBERT (*moves towards* DAVID). Let me see him.

ANNE. Don't touch him.

ROBERT. Of course. Sorry.

ANNE. This is the first he has been free of pain.

ROBERT. How did it happen?

WILLIAM. He was ambushed.

SAMUEL. Some of the surviving Unitedmen were running away from the battle.

ROBERT. A coward did this.

SAMUEL. They were at the end of the street. David was the first to chase after them.

ANNE. William is going to accompany Harry and they'll return with a physician.

ROBERT. What physician?

SAMUEL. Apparently our United friend here knows where a physician is hiding.

WILLIAM. Fortunately for him or he'd be dead already.

ANNE. And fortunately for us.

RUTH. Did you hear what he said, Father?

ROBERT. I heard him.

RUTH. You can't let him go with Harry.

SAMUEL. I have given him his orders and they do not include harming anyone.

ROBERT. If nobody objects I'll relieve him of his duty.

DAVID *moans as the pain wakes him.*

ANNE. David?

ROBERT. Are you all right, son?

DAVID. Father is that you?

ROBERT. It is.

DAVID. What do you think of this?

ROBERT. I think it will be better when Harry and I return.

DAVID. Harry?

ANNE. Try not to talk, son.

HARRY (*waiting at the door*). Sir!

ROBERT. I'm going to have to leave you.

ROBERT *kisses* DAVID *on the head before attempting to follow* HARRY *to the door.* SAMUEL *blocks his path.*

SAMUEL. I can't let you go, Robert.

ROBERT. What are you talking about?

SAMUEL *points his pistol directly at* ROBERT.

SAMUEL. Go back and comfort your son, Robert. Leave this business to me.

ROBERT. My son needs help.

SAMUEL. I know he does and I am going to make sure he gets it. You have to trust me, Robert.

ROBERT. I do trust you, but I do not trust two men, who already have good reason to quarrel, to travel together at speed and return safely with a physician.

RUTH. If both of them leave here, one of them will probably need a physician before they get where they are going.

ROBERT. Is that what you want?

DAVID. Is that Ruth?

DAVID *tries to stand. Everyone turns as* ANNE *tries desperately to prevent him from standing up.*

ANNE. Sit down, son. Sit down.

SAMUEL. Ruth, you're being called.

RUTH. I'm here, David.

DAVID. Is it your Harry they've been talking about? Is it?

RUTH. It is.

SAMUEL *takes another pistol from his coat and passes it to* WILLIAM.

SAMUEL. William, take this.

DAVID *moans in agony and then passes out.*

ANNE. He's all right, he's all right.

ROBERT. Let us go. Please.

SAMUEL. He's a strong boy, but he will need you here to help him survive until William returns.

WILLIAM. Let's go.

RUTH. Don't go, Harry. They only want you to lead them to the camp. Once they're there . . .

SAMUEL. Be quiet!

ROBERT. Tell me what your intentions are.

SAMUEL. My priority here is my soldier. Your son. This man claims that he will go and get a physician. I need William to accompany him.

RUTH. No you don't. My father could go.

SAMUEL. Your father can't keep him safe.

ROBERT. I could.

SAMUEL. I'm sorry, Robert, the truth is. You can't.

RUTH. I doubt that the truth has ever come from your lips.

ANNE. Ruth!

WILLIAM. Ruth, David's my friend.

ROBERT. Harry?

HARRY. What?

ROBERT. What say you?

WILLIAM. It has nothing to do with him.

ROBERT. Of course it has, if he refuses to go my son will die.

SAMUEL. Is that what you want, Ruth?

ROBERT. Ruth, think about your brother.

ANNE. This is my Grandson. He's bleeding to death. Please, someone make a decision.

SAMUEL. The decision's been made.

RUTH. Don't do it, Harry.

ANNE. Ruth!

RUTH. You stay here Harry until they agree to let you go alone or let my father go with you.

DAVID *moans louder.* ROBERT *returns to his son's side.*

ROBERT. Stay still son.

DAVID. I killed a Johnston today. (*Pause.*) You know what?

ROBERT. What?

DAVID. I wish with all my heart that I hadn't. I wish with all my life that he was still alive and that he was sitting here with us. What do you think of that?

ROBERT. That's good, son.

DAVID. But he's not here. He's not anywhere. He's dead. He's dead because I killed him.

ROBERT. Don't think about it.

DAVID. Do you forgive me?

ROBERT. Of course I do.

ANNE. Don't talk about it.

SAMUEL. You did what you had to do, son and you did it well.

DAVID. I wish I hadn't.

RUTH. So do I.

ANNE. Be quiet, Ruth.

SAMUEL. Are you going to side with the Unitedmen against your own family?

DAVID. This man, can you hear me?

ANNE. I can hear you sweetheart.

DAVID. This man was just standing there. You see we had them captured. The Grand Master had drawn up a great plan and explained it all to us and we did it, to the word, isn't that right?

SAMUEL. To the word.

ROBERT. Will you let us go?

DAVID. We killed them all. It was easy.

RUTH. I can't listen to this.

DAVID. Ruth! It was too easy, Ruth. Do you hear me?

RUTH. I'm not listening.

DAVID. Are you listening? You have to listen.

ANNE. I'm listening.

DAVID. He was shocked. Johnston, the sort of teacher fellow? It was his brother. Or cousin, I think. He was so shocked, you should have seen the look on his face and I looked down and saw my blade. It was right through him. Right through him.

ANNE. Don't talk about it any more, David. Drink this.

DAVID. No. No, I want you to hear me. I want Ruth to hear me. Ruth? Ruth, are you listening to me?

ANNE. Ruth, listen to him.

RUTH. I can't.

HARRY. Listen to him.

DAVID. I'm going to die.

ANNE. You're not.

DAVID. I am. I deserve it.

SAMUEL. Few deserve to live more than you, son.

ROBERT. If you believe that then why are you preventing us from getting him help?

DAVID. No, no, you're wrong.

ANNE. Don't talk like that.

SAMUEL. It's the wound talking.

DAVID. It is not. It's me!

DAVID *moans in agony.*

SAMUEL. It was too much for him.

RUTH. Let Harry go quickly.

SAMUEL. Where is this camp?

HARRY. It's a secret place.

SAMUEL. Where?

HARRY. It has all the supplies we will need, but if I wait here too long they may have to move.

ROBERT. Let us go now.

WILLIAM. And what if he brought armed men back with him?

HARRY. I give you my word, I will bring only a physician.

ROBERT. I believe him.

ANNE. You have to believe him.

WILLIAM. Father he could bring reinforcements.

DAVID. The pain, the pain . . .

ANNE *wipes his forehead with the water.*

HARRY. I must go at once.

SAMUEL. I think not.

DAVID. Father!

RUTH. Let Harry go.

HARRY. If I don't go now, he may die. Do you want another death on your hands?

DAVID. Father, I don't want to die. I'm really scared. Hold me.

ROBERT *moves back towards* DAVID.

ANNE. Pray with me?

DAVID. I don't think there is a God. I've seen things.

ANNE. You're all right, you've been dreaming.

DAVID *screams in agony.*

DAVID. I've seen terrible things. I think I've seen the devil. Am I going to die and go to hell?

ANNE. David, listen to me.

DAVID. Jesus Christ, help me. I don't want to go to hell. Father, keep me here.

A final scream and then silence. ANNE *holds him tight.*
RUTH *stands still.* ANNE *begins to rock* DAVID *to and fro.*

ANNE. There, there, love. No more pain.

RUTH (*to* SAMUEL). You caused this.

> ROBERT *checks the body.* DAVID *is dead.*

SAMUEL. Is he dead?

> ROBERT *turns in a rage.*

ROBERT. Why didn't you let us go?

SAMUEL. Many men have lost their sons today, Robert.

ROBERT. Because of people like you.

> ROBERT *attempts to cross the room obviously to attack*
> SAMUEL. WILLIAM *slams him on the head from behind.*
> *He falls to the ground.* RUTH *stands.*

ANNE. What are you doing?

RUTH. William, you're a bastard.

HARRY. Ruth!

ANNE. Why did you do that?

RUTH. You better go now, Harry!

SAMUEL. You're going nowhere. I need to know where this
    camp is.

RUTH. You see, Harry. That's all they wanted.

HARRY. I can't tell you that.

WILLIAM. What'll we do?

SAMUEL. We're going to get some answers.

ANNE. What are you going to do now?

SAMUEL. This man has information that I need.

RUTH. And when he supplies it and you need him no more, then
    what?

ANNE. Sir, I beg you. I have seen this man commit a great act
    of courage. He could have stayed hidden, but he revealed
    himself to try and help my grandson.

SAMUEL. I don't want any more trouble. But I do need to know
    where this camp is. Please tell me where it is.

HARRY. Sir, I can't do that.

WILLIAM. Tell us!

> RUTH *tries to bring* ROBERT *round.*

RUTH. Father, wake up!

SAMUEL. Well?

HARRY. I have even less reason to tell you anything than I had when the lad was still alive.

SAMUEL hits HARRY in the chest, knocking him backwards.

SAMUEL. How do you like pain for a reason?

RUTH turns from her father and rushes towards SAMUEL. WILLIAM grabs her and they wrestle.

ANNE. Harry, please tell them what they want to know. Please?

HARRY stands still as RUTH breaks free from WILLIAM.

RUTH. If you let Harry go, I will take you to the camp.

HARRY (*tries to hide his anger/disappointment*). Ruth?

WILLIAM. Don't listen to her, Father.

RUTH. I'm sorry, Harry.

WILLIAM. She's a liar, I should know.

RUTH. You never knew me at all.

HARRY. Sir, I must say that your behaviour here is a disgrace to your name and to your organisation. To the God you profess and indeed to the king you claim to serve. I surrendered myself to you in order to help this man and now I am to be your prisoner?

SAMUEL shoots HARRY through the chest and draws his sword all in one move. RUTH screams. WILLIAM stands in shock as HARRY falls to his knees.

RUTH grabs HARRY and tries to hold him upright.

SAMUEL. William, go outside and get ropes.

WILLIAM. What do you mean?

SAMUEL. At once!

WILLIAM leaves and SAMUEL checks outside for movement.

RUTH. Harry, don't leave me. Harry! I wasn't going to tell them. Harry please.

RUTH screams a terrible scream of passion and misery as she hugs HARRY, who has died in her arms.

ANNE. God save us. Lord help us.

> RUTH *kisses* HARRY *full on the mouth before* SAMUEL *pulls her away.* HARRY*'s body flops to the ground.* RUTH *jerks her arm free and rushes to the bedroom.*

SAMUEL. Where are your weapons?

ANNE. Weapons? What are you talking about?

SAMUEL. Are there weapons in that room?

ANNE. There are no weapons in this house apart from the ones that you brought.

> WILLIAM *returns with the ropes as* SAMUEL *surveys the situation and then begins to drag* ROBERT *out of the living room.* WILLIAM *assists him and they take* ROBERT *to the loom.*

WILLIAM. Where's Ruth?

SAMUEL (*the ropes*). They're for her. We'll have to tie him to this. (*The loom.*)

WILLIAM. How?

> SAMUEL *rips the loom and they use* ROBERT*'s own linen to tie him to it before returning to the living room.*

WILLIAM. What have I to do with these?

SAMUEL. The short one is for her hands the other throw over the beam and fasten it down.

> ROBERT *begins to come round and realises his predicament.*

WILLIAM. Where is she?

SAMUEL. She's in there! Now go do as you're bid.

> WILLIAM *does so.*

ANNE. Haven't you done enough?

SAMUEL. I intend to do what must be done. Your granddaughter has information that we require for the good of our country and our King. I have to get that information. Of you I ask only for your stillness and forgiveness.

ROBERT. Why am I tied?

> WILLIAM *fixes the rope over the beam and fastens it down.*

ANNE. Please don't harm my granddaughter.

ROBERT. Samuel! William!

WILLIAM. How are we going to get her out?

SAMUEL. Give me the pistol and make a noose on the end of that rope. Tie the other end . . .

WILLIAM. I know the procedure.

ROBERT. William!

ANNE. Please, I beg of you. Please, William talk to your father.

ROBERT. What's going on? What are you's doing? William!

SAMUEL. Ruth, would you come back in please?

ANNE. Climb out the window and escape, Ruth.

SAMUEL. Ruth, come back in or I'll shoot your grandmother in the head.

ROBERT *struggles violently.*

ROBERT. What the hell are you talking about, Samuel?

ANNE. Please, please stop and think about what you're doing.

SAMUEL. Ruth! I will count down from five and if I do not see you standing here in front of me you will not see her alive ever again. Five!

ANNE. William, don't do this. You loved Ruth, I know you did.

SAMUEL. Four!

ROBERT. Will somebody please help me out of this?

SAMUEL. Three!

ANNE. William, (*Pointing at* HARRY.) it was his fault. Why punish Ruth?

SAMUEL. Two!

RUTH *opens the door slowly and returns to the living room.* WILLIAM *grabs at her arms forcing them behind her back and ties them.*

RUTH. You don't need to tie me up. I neither intend to escape or cause you any trouble.

ANNE. Ruth . . .

As ANNE *begins to stand* SAMUEL *flashes his blade in front of her chest.*

SAMUEL. Please stay seated.

RUTH. Just close your eyes and pray.

SAMUEL. William, can I trust you to be strong enough for this?

WILLIAM. Yes.

SAMUEL. Place the noose around her neck.

RUTH. When you killed Harry you killed any chance of me telling you what you want to know.

ANNE. See William, how this man has spellbound her.

ROBERT. What's happening? What are you's doing?

SAMUEL. Ruth, please tell us all you can.

RUTH. No.

SAMUEL. Jerk the rope, William.

ROBERT. What rope? William?

ANNE. Please don't!

RUTH. Do what you will, you are only wasting time.

ROBERT. Ruth, what are you doing?

ANNE. Listen to her. She speaks as a woman possessed.

SAMUEL. She possesses information we need. Where is the secret meeting place, Ruth?

Silence but for ROBERT*'s struggling and moaning.*

ROBERT. Ruth, tell them anything they need to know.

SAMUEL. I'll ask you again, Ruth.

RUTH. Ask me as many times as you want.

SAMUEL. William, the rope again. Now, I'll give you a few seconds to consider your foolishness.

ROBERT. William!

ANNE. Tell them what they want, Ruth. What good will this do Harry now that he is dead?

WILLIAM. Just tell us, Ruth and we'll go.

ANNE. Can you not see how she has changed, William? You call these men demons. Are demons not capable of changing the hearts and minds of the innocent?

Silence. Still ROBERT *yells and screams.*

ANNE. Think about it. How could she have changed so much in so short a time? It is his influence, William, I mean it! Think about it.

Still silence as ANNE *waits for a response.*

ANNE. William, look in her eyes and tell me honestly that you can't see a change.

WILLIAM. Father, what say you?

SAMUEL. I say that this is her last chance.

ANNE. Ruth?

RUTH. Close your eyes and pray. I wish with all my heart that you did not have to see your grandchildren die.

ROBERT. Ruth! For God's sake, Ruth.

ANNE. Are you going to pray with me?

RUTH. I can pray only this.

ROBERT gives his all and nearly destroys the loom but eventually he is almost still and crying.

ANNE. Men! Let her pray and see if God will change her heart?

RUTH. Our Father who art in Heaven. Please forgive them for they know – nothing at all.

SAMUEL. If you don't tell me when I ask you again, before you die, you will see your Grandmother die.

SAMUEL points the gun at ANNE's head.

ANNE. Ruth, I would rather you saw me die, than I see you die.

ROBERT. Samuel, have you no heart?

RUTH. Then I'll see you in heaven. And damn you all to hell.

SAMUEL. Now I'll ask you for the last time. Where is this camp?

ROBERT. Don't do it, Samuel. Tell him Ruth.

Silence.

SAMUEL. You would let me do it too, wouldn't you? I hope you remember that, Anne. Kick the stool, William.

WILLIAM. What?

SAMUEL. Kick the stool. We're finished here.

ANNE. Well if you're finished here, why don't you just go.

ROBERT. What's happening, Mother? What are you saying?

SAMUEL. Kick the stool, William.

WILLIAM. She might be possessed, Father.

SAMUEL. William, this is an order. Kick the stool.

ANNE. William, don't.

SAMUEL. Kick the stool!

WILLIAM. Ruth, it's me William, can you hear me?

RUTH *laughs loudly.* ROBERT *screams.*

WILLIAM. Look at her, Father. Can you see any demons beating in her heart?

SAMUEL. She is no less than a demon herself. Kick the stool for God's sake.

ANNE. No!

WILLIAM. Ruth, this is your last chance.

SAMUEL. William!

WILLIAM. Father, I think this is something different.

ANNE. It's the work of demons.

SAMUEL. William, I know how much you loved her, son.

RUTH. William?

WILLIAM. What?

RUTH. Come here.

WILLIAM. What? What is it?

RUTH. Come closer.

SAMUEL. William stay where you are. What devilry is this?

WILLIAM. What is it Ruth?

SAMUEL. William do as you're told.

RUTH. I hope you love the world you're creating. I have no wish to see it so.

RUTH *steps off the stool and kicks it from under herself.* WILLIAM *grabs at her legs. She kicks at him.* ANNE *screams.* ROBERT *almost manages to stand but fails.*

WILLIAM. Help me, Father! Help me!

SAMUEL. Let her go, son!

WILLIAM. Father, please!

SAMUEL. Let her go!

SAMUEL *drags* WILLIAM *away from* RUTH. *Her body swings to and fro.* ROBERT *screams a terrible scream.*

WILLIAM. No!

SAMUEL. Get a hold of yourself. She and all her friends have caused a great many people to die today. Your family, your friends. Think about David. Look at him, don't look at her, look at him. William!

ANNE. God save us, no please, no!

WILLIAM. What have we done?

SAMUEL. We have brought these people to justice, William. And outside these walls there remains much work to be done if we are to preserve Ireland as we wish it to be. Now, get yourself together and follow me.

ANNE. Bastards! Bastards!

SAMUEL *flashes his blade towards* ANNE.

SAMUEL. Don't provoke me. What we've done here had to be done. Now, I'm very sorry for your loss. David in particular, but you were here and you witnessed the same as I.

ANNE. I witnessed murder, that's what I witnessed.

ROBERT. What have you done?

WILLIAM. What'll I do about Robert?

SAMUEL. She may untie him when we leave.

ANNE. You're a brave man standing there with a gun in one hand and a sword in the other.

WILLIAM *goes into the loom and begins to untie* ROBERT.

ROBERT. What have you done, William?

SAMUEL. You had a United Irishman in your house. Aiding traitors. That is treason itself and if you're not very careful you will find yourself on the end of a rope. Just like your granddaughter.

WILLIAM *has untied* ROBERT. ROBERT *stands. He rushes into the living room and in horror he goes to* RUTH *and struggles in an attempt to take her body down.* WILLIAM *tries to help him, he forces* WILLIAM *away.* ANNE *trembles as she offers a feeble attempt to help* ROBERT. ROBERT *manages to take her down and cradles her in his arms.*

SAMUEL. William, our work is done here.

ROBERT *continues to sob as he holds* RUTH. ANNE *tries to comfort him.*

SAMUEL. Come on, son.

WILLIAM. What can we do?

ROBERT. Get out!

WILLIAM. Father, make it not so.

SAMUEL. Just come with me, William.

ANNE. Go on, get out.

SAMUEL. William, I'm telling you for the last time.

WILLIAM. Father?

SAMUEL. What?

Pause.

What is it that you think? What is it that makes this any different to what there is out there? Today we have seen mothers lose sons, daughters lose fathers and much, much more. This! This is just harder because you thought these people were your friends. Your real friends are out there. Some dead, but many still alive and waiting to rebuild this whole country. Come with me now before I burn this place to the ground with all of you inside it.

SAMUEL *and* WILLIAM *leave.* ANNE *holds* DAVID *in her arms.* ROBERT *carries* RUTH'*s body to her. They embrace on the floor, mumbling prayers and crying.*

The End.